Graded examples in mathematics

CW01597478

Revisic..
of Topics
for GCSE
Answers

M. R. Heylings M.A., M.Sc.

Schofield & Sims Limited Huddersfield

0 7217 2340 3

First printed 1987
Reprinted 1988
Reprinted 1990

The series **Graded examples in mathematics** comprises:

Fractions and Decimals	0 7217 2323 3
Answer Book	0 7217 2324 1
Algebra	0 7217 2325 x
Answer Book	0 7217 2326 8
Area and Volume	0 7217 2327 6
Answer Book	0 7217 2328 4
General Arithmetic	0 7217 2329 2
Answer Book	0 7217 2330 6
Geometry and Trigonometry	0 7217 2331 4
Answer Book	0 7217 2332 2
Negative Numbers and Graphs	0 7217 2333 0
Answer Book	0 7217 2334 9
Matrices and Transformations	0 7217 2335 7
Answer Book	0 7217 2336 5
Sets, Probability and Statistics	0 7217 2337 3
Answer Book	0 7217 2338 1
Revision of Topics	0 7217 2339 x
Answer Book	0 7217 2340 3

Designed by Graphic Art Concepts, Leeds
Printed in England by Pindar Print Limited, Scarborough, North Yorkshire

Contents

Decimals

Part 1 Introduction

		(i)	(ii)
1	a	$\frac{3}{10}$	0.3
	b	$\frac{9}{10}$	0.9
	c	$\frac{7}{100}$	0.07
	d	$\frac{3}{100}$	0.03

2 **a** $\frac{5}{10} + \frac{2}{10} = \frac{52}{100} = 0.52$
b $\frac{2}{10} + \frac{9}{100} = \frac{29}{100} = 0.29$
c $\frac{7}{10} + \frac{5}{100} = \frac{75}{100} = 0.75$
d $\frac{1}{10} + \frac{6}{100} = \frac{16}{100} = 0.16$

3 **a** 0.76 **b** 0.382 **c** 0.817
d 0.604 **e** 0.053 **f** 0.902

4 **a** $\frac{7}{10}$ **b** $\frac{7}{100}$ **c** $\frac{31}{100}$ **d** $\frac{89}{100}$ **e** $\frac{3}{1000}$ **f** $\frac{31}{1000}$

		X	Y
5	a	1.4°C	31.8°C
	b	2.6°C	32.7°C

6 **A** 0.7 **B** 1.3 **C** 1.9 **D** 2.1 **E** 2.75 **F** 7.5 **G** 7.6
H 7.55 **I** 7.8 **J** 7.9 **K** 7.85 **L** 3.5 **M** 3.9 **N** 3.95
O 4.1 **P** 3.1 **Q** 3.05 **R** 2.9 **S** 2.95

7 1.45 kg 12.23 kg

Part 2 Problems

1 £17·99
2 4.5 litres
3 1.3 metres
4 £24·51
5 £4·74
6 £152·28
7 1740 kilocalories
8 £14·44
9 111 km
10 £26·54
11 £15·92, £3·98 each
12 £196·40
13 26.25 m²
14 3.25 kg

15

	1000	100	10	1	·	$\frac{1}{10}$	$\frac{1}{100}$	$\frac{1}{1000}$
a		1	7	8				
b		9	4	2				
c				0	·	6	7	
d				0	·	0	3	4
e		7	3	0				
f	1	2	5	0				
g				6	·	7	2	
h				0	·	1	9	5

16 **a** 4.2 grams
b 6.25 grams
c 270 grams
d 280 cm²
e 0.487 cm³/min
f 1025 grams

17 **a** 100 **b** 10
c 100 **d** 10
e 100 **f** 10 000
g 100 **h** 10 000

Fractions

Part 1 Equivalence, addition and subtraction

		(i)	(ii)	(iii)
1	**a**	$\frac{5}{21}$	$\frac{5}{21}$	$\frac{11}{21}$
	b	$\frac{1}{10}$	$\frac{3}{10}$	$\frac{6}{10}$
	c	$\frac{1}{8}$	$\frac{5}{8}$	$\frac{2}{8}$
	d	$\frac{5}{23}$	$\frac{11}{23}$	$\frac{7}{23}$

2 $\frac{9}{14}$ **3** $\frac{12}{35}$ **4** $\frac{89}{592}$

5 **a** $2\frac{1}{2}$ **b** $1\frac{3}{5}$ **c** $7\frac{1}{3}$ **d** $6\frac{1}{4}$ **e** $12\frac{3}{4}$

6 **a** $\frac{1}{2} = \frac{2}{4} = \frac{4}{8} = \frac{8}{16} = \frac{16}{32}$ **b** $\frac{1}{4} = \frac{2}{8} = \frac{4}{16} = \frac{8}{32}$ **c** $\frac{3}{4} = \frac{6}{8} = \frac{12}{16} = \frac{24}{32}$
d $\frac{1}{8} = \frac{2}{16} = \frac{4}{32}$ **e** $\frac{5}{8} = \frac{10}{16} = \frac{20}{32}$

7 **a** 5 **b** $6\frac{3}{4}$ **c** 9 **d** 10
e $10\frac{1}{4}$ **f** $3\frac{1}{4}$ **g** $7\frac{1}{2}$ **h** $4\frac{1}{4}$
i $3\frac{1}{2}$ **j** $2\frac{3}{4}$ **k** $1\frac{3}{4}$ **l** $3\frac{3}{4}$
m $6\frac{1}{2}$ **n** $3\frac{5}{8}$ **o** $7\frac{5}{8}$ **p** $6\frac{7}{8}$
q $7\frac{1}{8}$ **r** $2\frac{1}{8}$ **s** $2\frac{3}{8}$ **t** $3\frac{5}{8}$
u $3\frac{3}{4}$

8 **a** $2\frac{1}{4}$ in **b** 3 in
c $1\frac{5}{8}$ in **d** $3\frac{7}{8}$ in

9 **a** $4\frac{7}{8}$ in **b** $5\frac{1}{8}$ in

10 **a** $2\frac{5}{8}$ in **b** 3 in
c $2\frac{1}{4}$ in **d** $4\frac{1}{2}$ in

11 **a** $3\frac{3}{4}$ in **b** $\frac{7}{8}$ in
c $1\frac{3}{8}$ in **d** $4\frac{3}{8}$ in
e $4\frac{7}{8}$ in

12 **a** $1\frac{3}{4}$ in **b** $1\frac{5}{8}$ in
c $1\frac{1}{2}$ in **d** $1\frac{5}{8}$ in
e 2 in **f** $2\frac{1}{8}$ in
g $3\frac{3}{4}$ in

13 **a** $p = 6\frac{1}{4}$ $q = 1\frac{3}{4}$
b $r = 4\frac{1}{8}$ $s = 1\frac{7}{8}$
c $t = 3\frac{7}{8}$ $u = 6\frac{5}{8}$

14 **a** $\frac{1}{2} = \frac{4}{8}$ **b** $\frac{1}{4} = \frac{3}{12}$
c $\frac{2}{3} = \frac{4}{6}$ **d** $\frac{3}{5} = \frac{12}{20}$

15

	a		b		c		d
circle	$\frac{1}{2}$	=	$\frac{2}{4}$	=	$\frac{3}{6}$	=	$\frac{4}{8}$
square	$\frac{2}{3}$	=	$\frac{4}{6}$	=	$\frac{6}{9}$	=	$\frac{8}{12}$

16 **a** $\frac{3}{4} = \frac{15}{20}$ **b** $\frac{5}{8} = \frac{15}{24}$ **c** $\frac{3}{5} = \frac{9}{15}$ **d** $\frac{7}{10} = \frac{35}{50}$
e $\frac{2}{3} = \frac{10}{15}$ **f** $\frac{5}{12} = \frac{25}{60}$ **g** $\frac{1}{2} = \frac{9}{18}$ **h** $\frac{5}{6} = \frac{40}{48}$

17 **a** $\frac{4}{7}$ **b** $\frac{3}{4}$ **c** $\frac{7}{10}$ **d** $\frac{3}{5}$
e $\frac{3}{8}$ **f** $\frac{1}{4}$ **g** $\frac{7}{10}$ **h** $\frac{5}{6}$

18 **a** $\frac{1}{3}$
b (i) $\frac{2}{9}$ (ii) $\frac{1}{12}$
c (i) $\frac{3}{10}$ (ii) $\frac{7}{10}$

19 **a** $\frac{7}{9}$ **b** $\frac{7}{10}$
c $\frac{13}{24}$ **d** $\frac{5}{12}$
e $\frac{17}{24}$ **f** $\frac{11}{12}$ **g** $\frac{2}{3}$
h $\frac{13}{20}$ **i** $\frac{7}{12}$ **j** $\frac{1}{2}$

20 **a** $\frac{11}{12}$ **b** $\frac{17}{18}$
c $\frac{1}{6}$ **d** $\frac{7}{15}$
e $\frac{11}{12}$ **f** $\frac{9}{10}$ **g** $\frac{27}{40}$
h $\frac{7}{18}$ **i** $\frac{9}{40}$ **j** $\frac{11}{20}$

Fractions

Part 2 Multiplication and division

1 $\frac{3}{8}$

2 **a** $\frac{8}{15}$ **b** $\frac{15}{28}$ **c** $\frac{3}{8}$
d $\frac{14}{15}$ **e** $\frac{5}{8}$ **f** $3\frac{3}{4}$
g $\frac{5}{14}$ **h** $\frac{1}{3}$ **i** $\frac{1}{6}$
j $\frac{1}{2}$ **k** 3 **l** 1

3 **a** 12 cm^2 **b** 12 cm^2 **c** $11\frac{2}{3}$ cm^2

4 **a** 3 cm^3 **b** 15 cm^3 **c** $10\frac{1}{2}$ cm^3

5 **a** $2\frac{1}{2}$ kg
b (i) 7 m^2 (ii) $10\frac{1}{2}$ m^2
c $\frac{1}{4}$ h

6 **a** 8 packets
b (i) 8 (ii) 6
(iii) 6 (iv) 9
(v) 7 (vi) 14

7 **a** 2 **b** 6 **c** $1\frac{4}{5}$ **d** $\frac{4}{9}$
e $\frac{3}{5}$ **f** $4\frac{2}{3}$ **g** 4 **h** $1\frac{1}{5}$

8 **a** $\frac{3}{10}$
b $\frac{3}{5}$
c 10 days

Part 3 Ratios and fractions of quantities

1 **a** £6·24 **b** £4·35 **c** 21.9 m
d 3.10 m **e** 8.96 litres **f** 3.72 kg

2 0.5 kg

3 **a** 425 **b** 170 **c** 85

4 £2050

5 6.72 m^3

6 **a** $\frac{3}{4}$
b $\frac{1}{4}$
c 3:1

7 3:1

8 4:1

9 18:1

10 **a** 4:3
b 4:5

11 **a** £4·28 and £12·84
b 7.8 litres and 39.0 litres
c 9.92 m and 14.88 m
d 13.4 kg, 26.8 kg and 93.8 kg

12 **a** 10 boys **b** 15 girls

13 **a** 312 **b** 520

14 **a** 34 hectares **b** 102 hectares

15 **a** 48 grams **b** 120 grams

Percentages

Part 1 Percentages, decimals and fractions

1 **a** 34% **b** 27% **c** 52% **d** 97%

2 **a** $\frac{2}{5}$ **b** $\frac{4}{5}$ **c** $\frac{1}{4}$ **d** $\frac{7}{20}$ **e** $\frac{1}{10}$
f $\frac{1}{20}$ **g** $\frac{1}{2}$ **h** $\frac{3}{4}$ **i** $\frac{9}{20}$ **j** $\frac{1}{8}$

3 **a** 26% **b** 54% **c** 24% **d** 84% **e** 15%
f 70% **g** 60% **h** 25% **i** 75% **j** $3\frac{1}{2}$%
k $37\frac{1}{2}$% **l** $62\frac{1}{2}$% **m** $33\frac{1}{3}$% **n** $66\frac{2}{3}$% **o** $22\frac{2}{9}$%
p $44\frac{4}{9}$% **q** $14\frac{2}{7}$% **r** $85\frac{5}{7}$% **s** $83\frac{1}{3}$% **t** $58\frac{1}{3}$%

4 **a** 0.67 **b** 0.32 **c** 0.06 **d** 0.02 **e** 1.45
f 84% **g** 3% **h** 167% **i** 96% **j** 0.5%

Part 2 Percentages of quantities

1 **a** £1747·20
b 20%

2 £30

3 £21

4 20%

5 12%

6 28 litres

7 112 trees

8 £57·60

9 **a** £23·50 **b** £493·50

10 $12\frac{1}{2}$%

11 $37\frac{1}{2}$%

12 **a** 343 cm^3 **b** 2107 cm^3

Percentages

13 **a** 15% **b** 85%
14 276 hectares
15 **a** 25% **b** 75%
16 **a** 4% **b** 96%
17 15%
18 £247
19 3942 copies
20 9%
21 **a** 18 km **b** $3\frac{1}{3}$%
22 £151 230

Part 3 Percentages in society

Discounts

1 **a** 12p
b 60p
c £3
d £8·40
e £12·30
f £16·12
g £74·12
h £89·76

2 **a** £3·60
b £11·70
c £10·32
d £3·20
e £4·20
f £20·02

3 **a** 16p **b** 28p **c** 60p **d** £1 **e** £1·05 **f** £2·70

Cost price and selling price

		Profit	*Selling price*
4	**a**	£14·40	£254·40
	b	£57·00	£437·00
	c	£183·36	£947·36
	d	£157·76	£650·76

5 **a** (i) Profit = £30 (ii) 20% **b** (i) Profit = £15 (ii) 25%
c (i) Profit = £70 (ii) 25% **d** (i) Loss = £18 (ii) 15%

6 **a** £0·90 **b** 20%
7 **a** $12\frac{1}{2}$% **b** £17·55
8 **a** £19·84
b £143·84
9 £1117·20
10 Tuesday £35·20
Wednesday £31·68

Inflation and Compound Interest

11

	£
Price in Jan. 1983	8400
Increase	+ 840
Price in Jan. 1984	9240
Increase	+ 924
Price in Jan. 1985	10 164
Increase	+ 1 016·40
Price in Jan. 1986	11 180·40

12

	£
Initial amount	1250
Interest	100
Total after 1 year	1350
Interest	+ 108
Total after 2 years	1458
Interest	+ 116·64
Total after 3 years	1574·64

13 £705·60
14 £4515·84
15 £5856·40
16 £1251·52

Percentage error

17 **a** 15 grams **b** 3%
18 **a** £3·60 **b** 25%
19 **a** 9%
b $12\frac{1}{2}$%

		A	*B*
20	**a**	1.8°C	3.6°C
	b	$3\frac{3}{4}$%	$12\frac{1}{2}$%

Estimation

Part 1 Appropriate units

1
- **a** hours
- **b** seconds
- **c** minutes
- **d** hours
- **e** seconds
- **f** hours
- **g** seconds
- **h** minutes
- **i** seconds
- **j** hours
- **k** seconds
- **l** seconds or minutes

2
- **a** tonnes
- **b** grams
- **c** grams
- **d** kilograms
- **e** kilograms
- **f** tonnes
- **g** grams
- **h** kilograms
- **i** grams
- **j** tonnes
- **k** grams
- **l** kilograms or tonnes

3
- **a** kilometres
- **b** centimetres
- **c** metres
- **d** centimetres
- **e** millimetres
- **f** kilometres
- **g** metres or kilometres
- **h** millimetres
- **i** kilometres
- **j** metres
- **k** centimetres or metres
- **l** metres

4
- **a** cm^2
- **b** cm^2
- **c** m^2
- **d** m^2
- **e** km^2
- **f** cm^2
- **g** km^2
- **h** mm^2
- **i** cm^2
- **j** mm^2
- **k** m^2
- **l** km^2

5
- **a** cm^3
- **b** m^3
- **c** litres
- **d** litres or m^3
- **e** m^3
- **f** cm^3
- **g** cm^3 or litres
- **h** m^3
- **i** m^3
- **j** m^3
- **k** litres
- **l** m^3

6
- **a** (ii)
- **b** (ii)
- **c** (ii)
- **d** (ii)
- **e** (iii)
- **f** (ii)
- **g** (i)
- **h** (ii)
- **i** (ii)
- **j** (ii)
- **k** (ii)
- **l** (i)
- **m** (ii)
- **n** (i)
- **o** (ii)
- **p** (ii)
- **q** (ii)
- **r** (ii)
- **s** (ii)
- **t** (ii)
- **u** (ii)
- **v** (ii)
- **w** (iii)
- **x** (ii)
- **y** (ii)
- **z** (ii)

7
- **a** yes
- **b** yes
- **c** no; 200 m
- **d** yes
- **e** yes
- **f** yes
- **g** no; 8 m
- **h** no; 2 cm^2
- **i** yes
- **j** yes
- **k** yes
- **l** yes
- **m** yes
- **n** no; 7 h
- **o** yes
- **p** no; 10 grams
- **q** no; 30 cm
- **r** no; 300 cm^2
- **s** yes
- **t** no; 8000 cm^3
- **u** no; 40 m^3
- **v** no; 400 km^2
- **w** no; 1 tonne
- **x** yes
- **y** no; 90 kg
- **z** yes

8
- **a** 3 m
- **b** 8 m
- **c** 2 m
- **d** $\frac{1}{2}$ litre
- **e** 10 litres
- **f** 45 litres
- **g** 3 m^2
- **h** 2 m^2
- **i** 350 cm^2
- **j** 500 grams
- **k** 100 grams
- **l** 45 kg ($\simeq$ 7 stone)
- **m** 1 tonne
- **n** 1 m^2
- **o** 35 km
- **p** 20 m
- **q** 1 cm^2
- **r** $\frac{1}{5}$ cm^3
- **s** 5 mm^2
- **t** $\frac{1}{5}$ litre
- **u** 9 tonnes
- **v** 80 m
- **w** 2 km
- **x** 100 km
- **y** 8 cm
- **z** 200 cm^3

9
- **a** no
- **b** no
- **c** no
- **d** yes
- **e** no
- **f** no
- **g** no
- **h** yes
- **i** no
- **j** yes

Estimation

Part 2 Length and area

1 **a** 5 cm **b** 7 cm **c** 9.5 cm **d** 10.8 cm **e** 3.4 cm **f** 4.2 cm **g** 2.1 cm **h** 3.5 cm

2 **a** 5.3 cm **b** 7.4 cm **c** 7.5 cm **d** 11.0 cm **e** 10.8 cm **f** 6.4 cm

3 **b** (i) 2.5 km (ii) 5.2 km (iii) 3.4 km (iv) 7.5 km (v) 4.5 km (vi) 2.1 km (vii) 3.8 km (viii) 1.9 km
d (i) 7 km (ii) 12.4 km (iii) 6.9 km (iv) 12.4 km (v) 12.9 km

4 **b** (i) 35 km (ii) 39 km (iii) 52 km (iv) 64 km (v) 84 km (vi) 105 km (vii) 79 km (viii) 78 km
d (i) 122 km (ii) 130 km (iii) 74 km (iv) 125 km

5 **b** (i) 250 km (ii) 970 km (iii) 200 km (iv) 770 km (v) 450 km (vi) 400 km (vii) 770 km (viii) 1050 km
d (i) 1280 km (ii) 1390 km (iii) 690 km (iv) 650 km (v) 970 km

6 **a** 9.4 m **b** 5.4 m **c** 12.6 m **d** 6.9 m

7 **a** 5 m **b** 5.1 m **c** 7.6 m **d** 16 m

8 **a** 10 cm^2 **b** 9 cm^2 **c** 5 cm^2 **d** 35 cm^2 **e** 11 cm^2 **f** 5 cm^2

9 **c** **Field X** 14.5 cm^2 **Field Y** 18 cm^2 **Field Z** 26.7 cm^2

10

	Area, cm^2	Area, 000 km^2
Western Australia	14.6	2336
Northern Territory	8.4	1344
South Australia	5.8	928
Queensland	11.0	1760
New South Wales	4.7	752
Victoria	1.1	176
Tasmania	0.4	64

Length of coastline $\simeq$ 37 cm = 148 000 km

Part 3 Making reasonable estimates

1	b	**8**	b	**15**	b	**22**	b	**29**	c	**36**	c
2	c	**9**	c	**16**	c	**23**	c	**30**	b	**37**	b
3	b	**10**	c	**17**	a	**24**	b	**31**	c	**38**	b
4	c	**11**	b	**18**	a	**25**	a	**32**	b	**39**	a
5	c	**12**	c	**19**	c	**26**	b	**33**	b	**40**	c
6	c	**13**	b	**20**	a	**27**	a	**34**	c	**41**	b
7	b	**14**	c	**21**	a	**28**	c	**35**	c		

42 **a** yes **b** yes
c yes **d** no; 25
e yes **f** no; 25
g no; 0.4 **h** yes
i yes **j** yes
k no; 2 **l** yes
m yes **n** no; 45
o yes **p** yes

Estimation

Part 4 Problems

Any numerical answers given below are only estimates. Any other reasonable estimates are acceptable.

1 no
2 yes
3 $4\frac{1}{2}$ hours
4 yes
5 yes
6 8 hours
7 20 m^2
8 **a** 26 m^2 **b** 1300
9 **a** 15 m^2 **b** £120
10 **a** 84 m^2 **b** £42
11 10 pence
12 9 pence
13 £3
14 90 pence
15 20 pence
16 £5 to £6
17 **a** 120 m^2 **b** £1200
18 **a** 400 m^2 **b** £1600
19 **a** 7 litres **b** £2·50
20 **a** 8 litres **b** £2·50
21 **a** 40 litres **b** £14
22 90

23 **a** 4 hours **b** 5 hours **c** $6\frac{1}{2}$ hours
24 **a** 3 cm^2 **b** 12 cm^2 **c** 75 cm^2
d 150 cm^2 **e** 300 cm^2 **f** 450 cm^2
25 **a** 80 **b** 1000
c 150
26 **a** 750 cm^3 **b** 300 cm^3
c 180 cm^3
27 229 cm^3 should be about 125 cm^3.
28 **a** 3 cm **b** 4 cm **c** 7 cm **d** 9 cm
29 **a** 3 **b** 5 **c** 1
30 3.01 should be about 8.
31 **a** $154 + 289 = 443$ **b** $847 - 592 = 255$
c $106 \times 12 = 1272$ **d** $32 \times 85 = 2720$
e $851 \div 23 = 37$ **f** $56 + 281 = 337$
g $389 + 472 - 256 = 605$ **h** $(109 + 17) \div 18 = 7$
i $(364 \times 4) - 21 = 1435$ **j** $(56 + 12) \times 3 = 204$
k $(112 - 96) \times 4 = 64$ **l** $(678 + 518) \div 92 = 13$
m $36 \times 14 \div 3 = 168$ **n** $976 \div 2 \div 8 = 61$
o $4 \times (406 + 31) = 1748$ **p** $(64 + 85 - 121) \times 4 = 112$
q $(894 \div 6) + 14 = 163$ **r** $(366 \times 16 \div 24) - 168 = 76$
32 **a** $22 \times 34 = 748$ **b** $23 \times 14 = 322$
c $42 \times 54 = 2268$ **d** $83 \times 47 = 3901$
e $76 \times 54 = 4104$ **f** $32 \times 54 = 1728$
g $45 \times 63 = 2835$ **h** $82 \times 29 = 2378$
i $54 \times 77 = 4158$ **j** $53 \times 72 = 3816$
k $81 \times 69 = 5589$ **l** $73 \times 98 = 7154$ *or* $78 \times 93 = 7254$
m $123 \times 56 = 6888$ **n** $333 \times 24 = 7992$
o $15 \times 23 \times 67 = 23\,115$

Approximation

Part 1 Rounding off

1 **a** 9.9 cm
b 10 cm
2 **a** (i) 19 cm (ii) 124 cm (iii) 10 cm (iv) 1 cm
b (i) 46 kg (ii) 369 kg (iii) 3 kg (iv) 13 kg
c (i) £6·20 (ii) £37·40 (iii) £0·60 (iv) £4·00
3 19 cm
4 21.8 cm
5 232 m

Approximation

		(i)	(ii)
6	a	1.6	1.65
	b	1.1	1.06
	c	0.095	0.09
	d	0.30	0.30

7 a 41 kg b 40.9 kg
c 40.9 kg

8 a 906 km b 910 km c 900 km

9 a 2 m^2 b 2.1 m^2
c 2.1 m^2 d 2.06 m^2

10 a 5 grams b 5.3 grams
c 5.27 grams d 5.3 grams

Part 2 Limits of accuracy

1 a £7·50 $\leqslant$ price $<$ £8·50 b £11·50 $\leqslant$ price $<$ £12·50
c £185 $\leqslant$ price $<$ £195 d £185 $\leqslant$ price $<$ £195

2 a 12.5 m $\leqslant$ length $<$ 13.5 m b 115 m $\leqslant$ length $<$ 125 m
c 6.35 m $\leqslant$ length $<$ 6.45 m d 2.935 m $\leqslant$ length $<$ 2.945 m

3 a 194.5 miles
b 191.5 miles

4 a 5.15 litres
b 4.85 litres

5 a 32.5°
b 31.5°

6 a 126 grams
b 124 grams

7 2600 cm^2 to 2700 cm^2

8 380 revs to 390 revs

9 2.1 m to 2.2 m

10 $52 \leqslant x \leqslant 91$
$3 \leqslant y \leqslant 13$
$11\frac{1}{2} \leqslant z \leqslant 33$

Indices

Part 1 Indices

1 a 2, 3, 5, 7, 11, 13, 17, 19
b (i) $2 \times 2 \times 3 \times 3 \times 5$
(ii) $2 \times 2 \times 2 \times 3 \times 7$
(iii) $2 \times 3 \times 3 \times 5 \times 11$
(iv) $2 \times 2 \times 2 \times 2 \times 2 \times 3 \times 3 \times 3 \times 3 \times 13$
c (i) $2^2 \times 3^2 \times 5$
(ii) $2^3 \times 3 \times 7$
(iii) $2 \times 3^2 \times 5 \times 11$
(iv) $2^5 \times 3^4 \times 13$

2 a 64 b 36 c 12 d 81 e 64
f 12 g 200 h 2700 i 16

3 a 2^{11} b 3^{10} c 5^{11}
d 2^5 e 3^6 f 4^4
g 8^7 h 4^6 i 6^{15}

4 a $n = 4$ b $n = 7$
c $n = 1$ d $n = 9$

5 a 19 683 b 59 049 c 2187

6 a 4800 b 392 000 c 10 500
d 480 000 000 e 56 700 f 970 000

7 a 3.7×10^4 b 6.4×10^8 c 5.24×10^4
d 1.3×10^5 km^2
e 3.84×10^5 km
f 1.42×10^8 miles

Indices

8

Power of 2	Its value
0	$2^0 = 1$
1	$2^1 = 2$
2	$2^2 = 4$
3	$2^3 = 8$
4	$2^4 = 16$
5	$2^5 = 32$
6	$2^6 = 64$
7	$2^7 = 128$
8	$2^8 = 256$
9	$2^9 = 512$
10	$2^{10} = 1024$
11	$2^{11} = 2048$
12	$2^{12} = 4096$

a 1024 **b** 4096
c 2048 **d** 1024
e 8 **f** 16
g 16 **h** 32

9
$1 \times 4 = 4$
$2 \times 4 = 8$
$4 \times 4 = 16$
$8 \times 4 = 32$
$16 \times 4 = 64$
$32 \times 4 = 128$
$64 \times 4 = 256$

Part 2 Roots and indices

1 $\sqrt{18} = 4.24$

2 **a** $\sqrt{24} = 4.90$
b $\sqrt{30} = 5.48$

3 **a** 3 **b** 4 **c** 7 **d** 9 **e** 10 **f** 20

4 **a** 5 cm
b 6 cm
c 2 cm
d 32 metres

5 **a** 1.87 m
b 39 cm
c 237 cm
d 23.7 m

6 $\sqrt[3]{20} = 2.71$

7 $\sqrt[3]{30} = 3.11$
$\sqrt[3]{100} = 4.64$

8 **a** (i) 2 (ii) 3 (iii) 4 (iv) 5 (v) 10
b 3 cm
c 2 m, 4 m^2

9 **a** (i) 4 (ii) 4
b $\frac{1}{16}$
c $\frac{1}{9}$ **d** $\frac{1}{25}$ **e** $\frac{1}{8}$ **f** $\frac{1}{1000}$ **g** $\frac{1}{32}$ **h** $\frac{1}{81}$ **i** $\frac{1}{64}$

10

	Without standard form	Using standard form
a	0.0095 cm	**9.5×10^{-3} cm**
b	**0.00015 cm^2**	1.5×10^{-4} cm^2
c	0.000000034 cm	**3.4×10^{-8} cm**
d	**0.00000059 cm**	5.9×10^{-7} cm
e	0.0025 kg	**2.5×10^{-3} kg**

11 **a** (i) 9 (ii) 9
b (i) 8 (ii) 8
c (i) 3 (ii) 2 (iii) 6 (iv) 9
(v) 10 (vi) 2 (vii) 2 (viii) 3

Proportion

a directly
b directly
c inversely
d inversely
e inversely
f inversely

Part 1 Direct proportion

1 a

Area, x m^2	1	2	3	4	5	10	15	20
Number, y	4	8	12	16	20	40	60	80

$y = 4x$

b

Flights, x	1	2	3	4	5	10	15	20
Cost, £y	80	160	240	320	400	800	1200	1600

$y = 80x$

c

Volume, x cm^3	1	2	3	4	5	10	15	20
Mass, y grams	1.2	2.4	3.6	4.8	6.0	12	18	24

$y = 1.2x$

2 45p **3** 500 boxes **4** \$23·80 **5** 134 km

Part 2 Inverse proportion

a

Time, x hours	1	2	3	4	5	6	10
Average speed, y mph	120	60	40	30	24	20	12

$y = \frac{120}{x}$

b

Number, x	1	2	3	4	5	6	10
Time, y hours	60	30	20	15	12	10	6

$y = \frac{60}{x}$

c

Number, x	1	2	3	4	5	6	10
Angle, $y°$	360	180	120	90	72	60	36

$y = \frac{360}{x}$

2 10 days **3** 20 hours **4** 60 minutes

A mixture

5 100 minutes **6** 12 days **7** 84 francs **8** £5·40 **9** 27 boxes **10** 40 mph

Part 3 Other types of proportion

1 a (i) 3 (ii) $y = 3x^2$
b (i) 2 (ii) $y = 2x^3$
c (i) 5 (ii) $y = 5\sqrt{x}$
d (i) 15 (ii) $y = \frac{15}{x}$
e (i) 9 (ii) $y = \frac{9}{x^2}$
f (i) 24 (ii) $y = \frac{24}{\sqrt{x}}$

2 a $y = 2t^2$ **b** 50
3 a $E = 4\omega^2$ **b** 16
4 a $v = 2\sqrt{r}$ **b** 10
5 a $F = \frac{36}{x^2}$ **b** 4

Changes of units

Part 1 Foreign exchange

1 **a** 5 Swiss fr. **b** 8 Swiss fr.
c 12 Swiss fr. **d** 6·50 Swiss fr.
e £4 **f** £3·40
g £2·60 **h** £4·60

2 **a** 400 esc. **b** 700 esc.
c 840 esc. **d** 1600 esc.
e £2·50 **f** £2·10
g £3·25 **h** £4·70
j better

3

Pounds sterling, £	1	2	3	4	5	8	10
Icelandic kronur, kr	60	120	180	240	300	480	600

a £7·50
b 510 kronur

4 **a** 20 580 dinars
b £7·43

5 Outward ticket is cheaper by 270 rupees (£14·36)

6 The first arrangement is cheaper by £28·91.

Part 2 Other conversions

1 **a** 44 lb
b 9680 lb
c Higgens 75 kg Müller 161 lb

2 **a** The plastic drum is 0.75 litres larger.
b 2.22 gallons; £20
c The second garage by 4.1 pence per gallon.

3 **a** 5 acres 8.5 acres
b 0.6 hectares

4 **a**

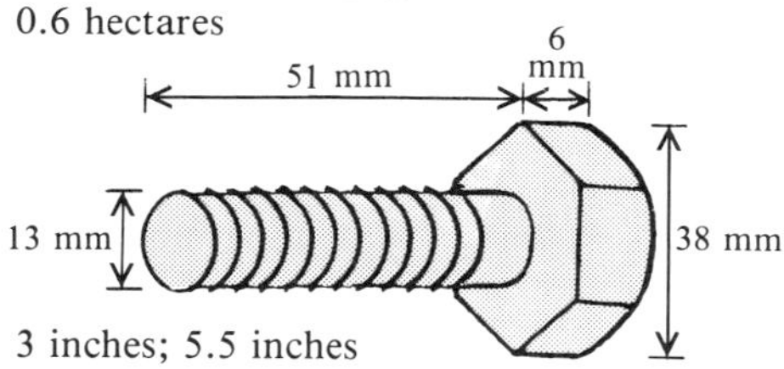

b 3 inches; 5.5 inches

5 **a** 432 miles; 510 miles; 659 miles
b 2 miles

6 **a** 20 litres **b** 40 litres **c** 50 litres **d** 70 litres

Part 3 Imperial and other units

1 25 strips; 2 inches left
2 12 oz
3 161 lb
4 3 h 45 min
5 48 lengths
6 36 bottles
7 1 lb 13 oz
8 1 ft 8 in

Perimeter

1 **a** **A** 7.8 cm
B 11 cm
b **A** 390 m
B 550 m

2 **a** 16 cm
b 32 m
c £14·72

3 **a** 12.2 cm
b 3050 m
c $1\frac{1}{2}$ h

4 **a** 14 cm **b** 22.2 cm
c 14 cm **d** 45 cm
e 9.8 cm

5 **a** $9\frac{1}{3}$ cm
b $9\frac{1}{4}$ cm
c 23 cm
d $27\frac{3}{5}$ cm

6 **a** 126 m
b 151 m

7 **a** 25.1 cm **b** 75.4 cm **c** 35.2 cm
d 132 cm **e** 22 cm **f** 66 cm

8 **a** 3.14 cm
b 9.14 cm

9 **a** $27\frac{1}{2}$ m
b $97\frac{1}{2}$ m

10 **a** 6.28 cm **b** 3.93 cm **c** 3.14 cm
d $14\frac{2}{3}$ cm **e** $15\frac{5}{7}$ cm **f** $2\frac{3}{4}$ cm

Area

Part 1 Introduction

1 1 – **A**
2 – **D**
3 – **C**
4 – **B**

2 All except **d**

3 **a** 6 cm^2 **b** 7 cm^2

4 **a** $3\frac{1}{2}$ cm^2 **b** 6 cm^2 **c** 5 cm^2

5 Anglesey 25.6 cm^2, Isle of Man 21.5 cm^2
a 1 cm^2 = 25 km^2
b Anglesey 640 km^2
Isle of Man 538 km^2

Part 2 Using formulae

1 **a** 96 cm^2 **b** 30 cm^2 **c** 63 cm^2 **d** 25 cm^2
e 50.2 cm^2 **f** 154 cm^2
g 48.9 cm^2 **h** 27.2 cm^2 **i** 45.8 cm^2 **j** 43.5 cm^2
k 55.4
l $17\frac{1}{2}$ cm^2 **m** $6\frac{2}{3}$ cm^2 **n** 20 cm^2
o $8\frac{3}{4}$ cm^2 **p** $38\frac{1}{2}$ cm^2

2 **a** 16 000 cm^2 = 1.6 m^2
b 14 300 cm^2 = 1.43 m^2

3 **a** 27.3 m^2
b 40.7 m^2
c 13.4 m^2

4 **a** 4
b 371.2 m^2
c 81.74 m^2
d 44.24 m^2

5 **a** 73 m^2
b 3500 bricks

6 489 mm^2

7 **a** 432 m^2
b 201 m^2
c 231 m^2

8 **a** 1.2 cm, 0.9 cm
b 2.54 cm^2
c 1.98 cm^2

Area

9 **a** 42 cm, 56 cm
b 154 cm^2
c 504 cm^2

10 **a** 18.8 cm^2 **b** 6.28 cm^2 **c** 9.42 cm^2
d 154 cm^2 **e** $15\frac{5}{7}$ cm^2 **f** $15\frac{2}{5}$ cm^2

11

England	10.5 cm^2
Scotland	1.2 cm^2
Wales	0.6 cm^2
N. Ireland	0.3 cm^2

12 11 km^2

Volume

Part 1 Cuboids

1 **a** (i) 12 (ii) 24
b (i) 15 (ii) 45
c (i) 24 (ii) 36

2 **a** (i) 26.0 cm^2 (ii) 62.4 cm^3
b (i) 7.0 cm^2 (ii) 32.2 cm^3
c (i) $2\frac{1}{2}$ cm^2 (ii) 4 cm^3
d (i) 21 cm^2 (ii) 14 cm^3

3 **a** 4908.6 cm^3; 5 litres
b $4\frac{1}{2}$ tins

4 **a** 2.5 litres
b 19 slabs

5 **a** 7.5 litres
b 40 seconds

Part 2 Prisms and cylinders

1 **a** (i) 15 cm^2 (ii) 105 cm^3 **b** (i) 36 cm^2 (ii) 144 cm^3 **c** (i) 24 cm^2 (ii) 120 cm^3

2 **a** 28 cm^2; 84 cm^3 **b** 80 cm^2; 400 cm^3
c 12.56 cm^2; 62.8 cm^3 **d** $38\frac{1}{2}$ cm^2; 308 cm^3

3 **a** 501.4 cm^3
b no

4 131 cm^3

5 **a** 1000 cm^3
b 915 cm^3

Part 3 Pyramids and cones

		Cuboid	Pyramid
1	**a**	240 cm^3	80 cm^3
	b	150 cm^3	50 cm^3
	c	252 cm^3	84 cm^3

2 **a** (i) 192 cm^2 (ii) 500 cm^3 **b** (i) 50.2 cm^2 (ii) 100 cm^3
c (i) 154 cm^2 (ii) 462 cm^3

3 **a** 36.4 m^2
b 103 m^3
c 144 tonnes

4 **a** 0.469 m^3
b 0.117 m^3

5 24.7 litres; 7.33 litres
Volume of bucket = 17.4 litres

Part 4 Spheres

1 **a** (i) 33.5 cm^3 (ii) 523 cm^3 (iii) 268 cm^3
b (i) $179\frac{2}{3}$ cm^3 (ii) $\frac{11}{21}$ cm^3 (iii) $14\frac{1}{7}$ cm^3

2 17 100 cm^3

3 **a** 16 747 + 2939 = 19 700 cm^3 to 3 significant figures
b 53.2 kg

Solids and nets

Part 1 Isometric drawings

1 $F + V - E = 2$ in all cases

2 **a** 360 cm **b** 600 cm **c** 580 cm

3 **a**

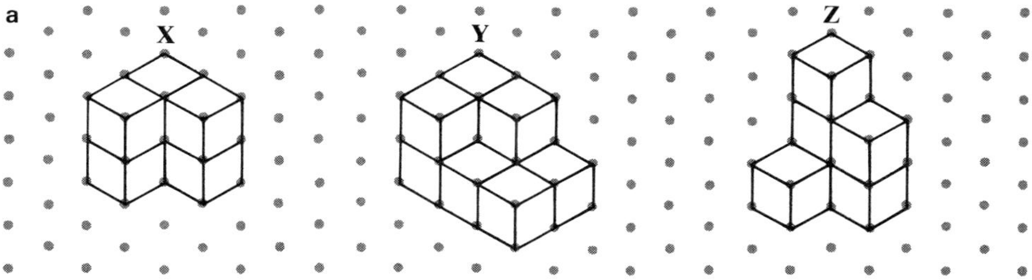

b

		X	Y	Z
(i)	Original solid	24 cm^2	32 cm^2	28 cm^2
(ii)	Final solid	22 cm^2	30 cm^2	24 cm^2

4

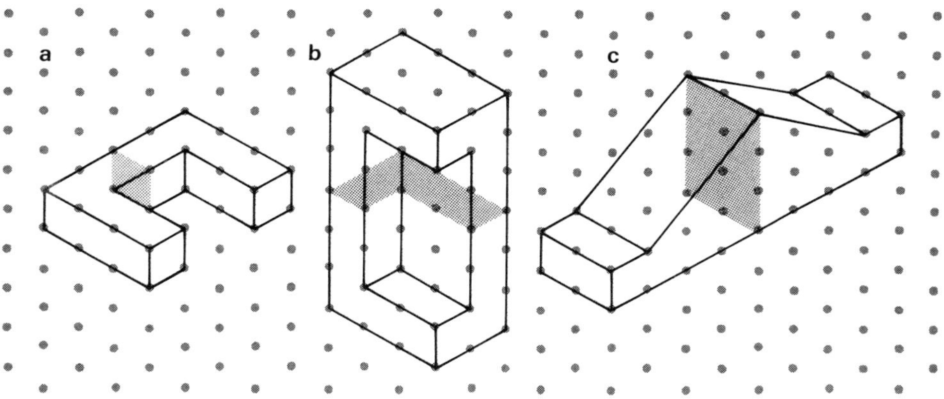

5

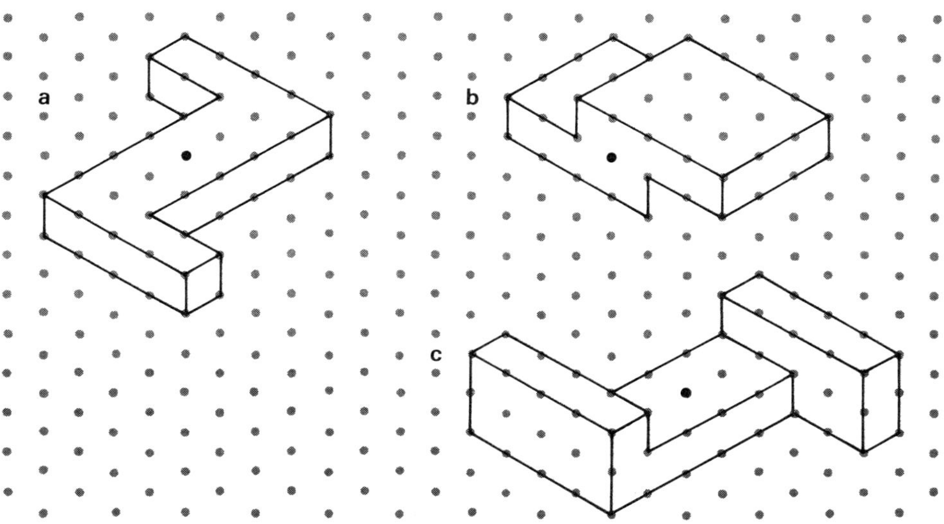

Solids and nets

Part 2 Nets and surface area

1 **a** 7
b 4
c *PQ* **d** *OP* **e** *JI* **f** *KJ*
g *I* **h** *P* **i** *N* **j** *M, C* and *E*

2 **a** *Y*
b 216 cm²

3 **a** 4
b *BC* and *CD*
c *K* and *M*

4 240 cm²

5 504 cm²

6 **a**

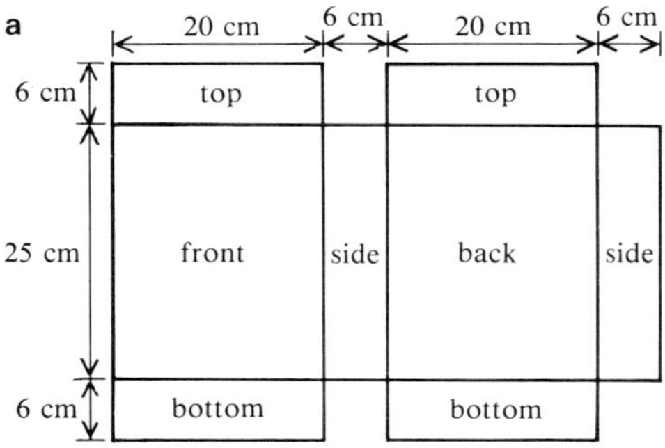

This net is only one of several possibilities.

b 1540 cm²
c 1924 cm²

7 **a**

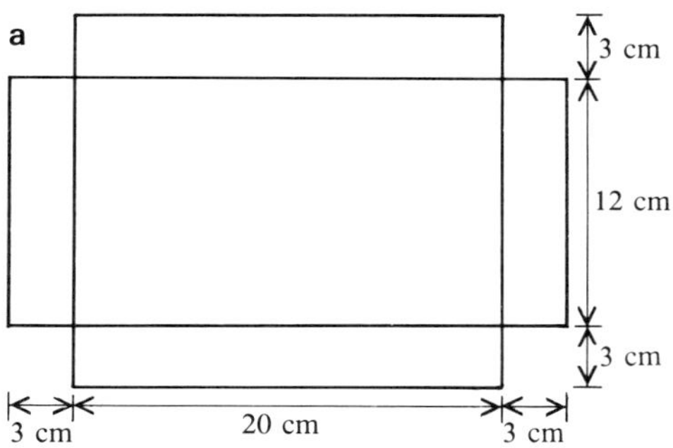

This net is that which provides the answer to part **b**.

b Smallest rectangle is 26 cm by 18 cm
Wasted area = 36 cm²
c 1312 cm²

8 314 cm²

9 **a** 880 cm²
b 1188 cm²

10 **a** 154 cm²
b 113 cm²

11 **a** 5024 cm²
b 129 cm²

12 628 + 314 + 251 = 1193 cm²

13 **a** 84.8 cm²
b 6 cm

14 1570 cm²

15 2826 cm²

Part 3 Plans and elevations

1 **a** a typewriter; side view **b** a kettle; front view **c** a lorry; top view

2 **a** *A* = *2*; *B* = *3*; *C* = *1*
b *A* = *3*; *B* = *1*; *C* = *2*

Solids and nets

3

a

plan

elevation

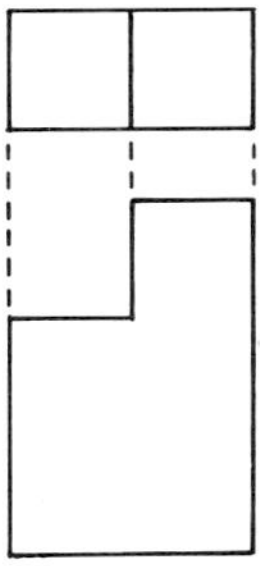

b

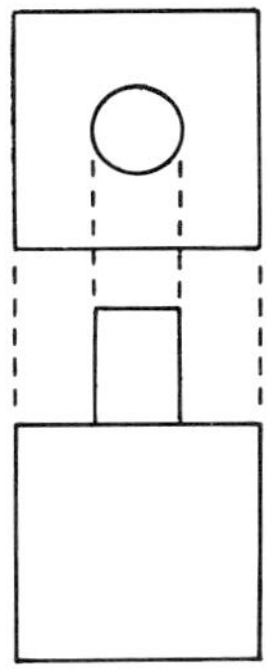

c

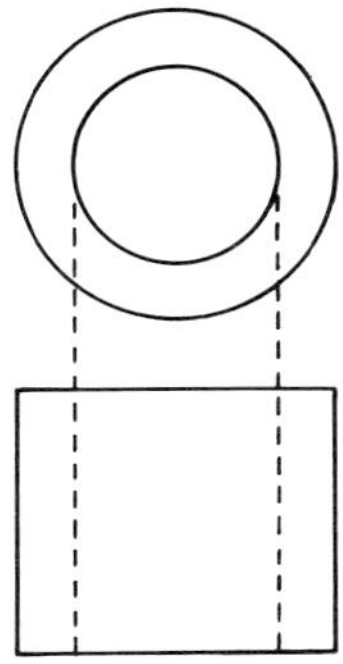

d

plan

elevation

e

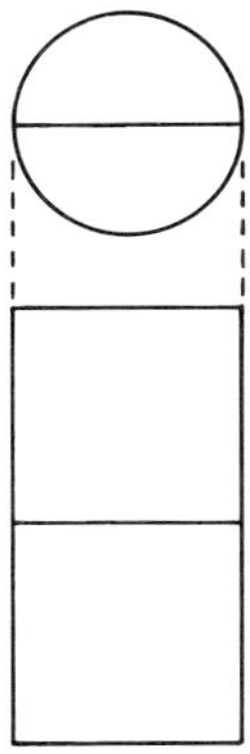

f

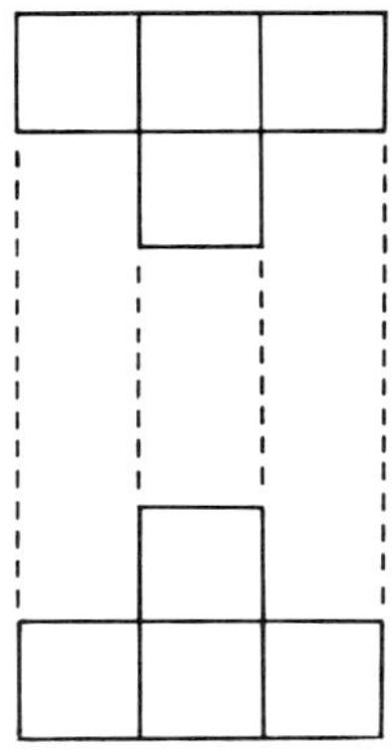

4 **a**

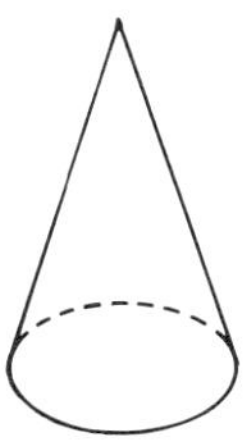

b

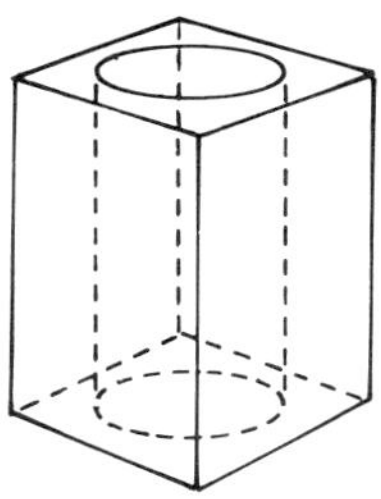

c

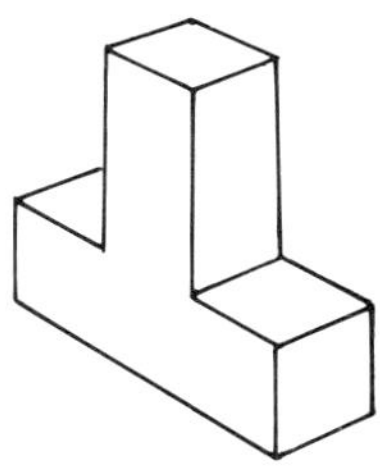

5 **b**

Angles

Part 1 Turns and bearings

1
- **a** 70°
- **b** 70°
- **c** 90°
- **d** 45°
- **e** 65°
- **f** 95°
- **g** 30°
- **h** 60°

2 **a**
- **a** = 30°
- **b** = 65°
- **c** = 80°
- **d** = 100°
- **e** = 135°
- **f** = 135°

b

1st leg 1.8 cm;	2.7 km
2nd leg 5 cm;	7.5 km
3rd leg 6 cm;	9 km
4th leg 6 cm;	9 km
5th leg 5.5 cm;	8.25 km
6th leg 5.4 cm;	8.1 km
7th leg 3.4 cm;	5.1 km
Total journey =	49.65 km

Angles

3 **a** 030°
b 050°
c 070°
d 160°
e 205°
f 230°
g 235°
h 350°
i 120°
j 140°
k 280°
l 300°
m 315°

4

Leg		Distance, km	Bearing
1st	G to T	30	090°
2nd	T to U	45	040°
3rd	U to V	51	130°
4th	V to W	60	200°
5th	W to X	42	260°
6th	X to Y	105	005°
7th	Y to Z	48	052°
8th	Z to B	90	260°

5 880 km; 159°

6 8.6 km; 058°

7 **a** 68 km **b** 46 km
c 053° **d** 186°

Part 2 Points, lines and shapes

1 **a** 120° **b** 120° **c** 210° **d** 130°

2 **a** 30° **b** 60° **c** 60° **d** 30°

3 **a** **i** = 130°, **j** = **k** = 50° **b** **l** = **n** = 120°, **m** = 60° **c** **o** = **r** = 40°, **p** = 90°, **q** = 50° **d** **s** = 70°, **t** = **u** = 40°

4 **a** **v** = 70°, **w** = 110° **b** **x** = **z** = 135°, **y** = 45° **c** **a** = 85°, **b** = 40° **d** **c** = 70°, **d** = 45°

5 **a** **e** = 85° **b** **f** = 70°, **g** = 40° **c** **h** = **i** = 30° **d** **j** = 30°, **k** = 120°, **l** = 60°, **m** = 80°

6 **a** **n** = 60°, **o** = 70°, **p** = 120°, **q** = 60° **b** **r** = 40°, **s** = 30°, **t** = 90° **c** **u** = **v** = 55°, **w** = 50°, **x** = 65°
d **y** = 70°, **z** = 55° **e** **a** = 120° **f** **b** = 30°
g **c** = 30°, **d** = 10° **h** **e** = 45°, **f** = 70°

7

Polygon	Number of sides	Number of triangles	Sum of all angles
Triangle	3	1	180°
Quadrilateral	4	2	360°
Pentagon	5	3	540°
Hexagon	6	4	720°
Heptagon	7	5	900°
Octagon	8	6	1080°
Nonagon	9	7	1260°
Decagon	10	8	1440°
Undecagon	11	9	1620°
Dodecagon	12	10	1800°

8 **a** 60° **b** 140° **c** 50° **d** 50°

9 170° each

10 **x** = 70°

11 **x** = 54°

12 **a** 108°
b (i) 135° (ii) 120° (iii) 144° (iv) 150°

Angles

Part 3 Angles in circles

1	**a**	$\mathbf{a} = 35^\circ$	**b**	$\mathbf{b} = 50^\circ$	**c**	$\mathbf{c} = 30^\circ$ $\mathbf{d} = 25^\circ$	**d**	$\mathbf{e} = 50^\circ$
2	**a**	$\mathbf{t} = 25^\circ$	**b**	$\mathbf{u} = 35^\circ$ $\mathbf{v} = 55^\circ$	**c**	$\mathbf{w} = \mathbf{x} = 60^\circ$	**d**	$\mathbf{y} = 70^\circ$ $\mathbf{z} = 20^\circ$
3	**a**	$\mathbf{a} = 70^\circ$ $\mathbf{b} = 40^\circ$	**b**	$\mathbf{c} = 60^\circ$ $\mathbf{d} = 30^\circ$	**c**	$\mathbf{e} = \mathbf{f} = 20^\circ$ $\mathbf{g} = \mathbf{h} = 50^\circ$	**d**	$\mathbf{i} = \mathbf{j} = 55^\circ$ $\mathbf{k} = \mathbf{l} = 45^\circ$
4	**a**	$\mathbf{m} = 110^\circ$	**b**	$\mathbf{n} = 50^\circ$ $\mathbf{p} = 100^\circ$	**c**	$\mathbf{q} = 110^\circ$ $\mathbf{r} = 220^\circ$	**d**	$\mathbf{s} = 25^\circ$ $\mathbf{t} = 50^\circ$
5	**a**	$\mathbf{a} = 80^\circ$ $\mathbf{b} = 100^\circ$	**b**	$\mathbf{c} = 75^\circ$ $\mathbf{d} = 105^\circ$ $\mathbf{e} = 60^\circ$	**c**	$\mathbf{f} = 115^\circ$ $\mathbf{g} = \mathbf{h} = 65^\circ$ $\mathbf{i} = 115^\circ$	**d**	$\mathbf{j} = 95^\circ$ $\mathbf{k} = 110^\circ$ $\mathbf{l} = 85^\circ$ $\mathbf{m} = 70^\circ$
6	**a**	$\mathbf{a} = 70^\circ$	**b**	$\mathbf{b} = 115^\circ$ $\mathbf{c} = 90^\circ$ $\mathbf{d} = 65^\circ$	**c**	$\mathbf{e} = 70^\circ$ $\mathbf{f} = 20^\circ$	**d**	$\mathbf{g} = 45^\circ$
	e	$\mathbf{h} = 50^\circ$ $\mathbf{i} = 20^\circ$	**f**	$\mathbf{j} = 60^\circ$ $\mathbf{k} = 30^\circ$	**g**	$\mathbf{l} = 40^\circ$ $\mathbf{m} = 50^\circ$	**h**	$\mathbf{n} = 75^\circ$
7	**a**	$\mathbf{y} = 90^\circ - \mathbf{x}$	**b**	$\mathbf{y} = \mathbf{x}$	**c**	$\mathbf{y} = 90^\circ - \mathbf{x}$	**d**	$\mathbf{y} = 90^\circ - 2\mathbf{x}$
8	$\lambda = 45^\circ$							
9	**a**	53°	**b**	$26\frac{1}{2}^\circ$				
10	**a**	45°	**b**	135°				
11	**a**	45°	**b**	45°				

Part 4 Constructions

1 **a** Height = 3.7 cm
Area = 14.8 cm^2

b XZ = 8 cm
Area = 32 cm^3

c Height = 6.1 cm
Area = 24.4 cm^2

2 AC = 61 m
BC = 35 m

3 **a** 8.7 km
b 10 km

4 16.1 km

5 2790 m^2 + 2340 m^2 = 5130 m^2

6 3.6 cm; 1.6 cm

7 50 cm

8 1.7 km

Scale drawings and loci

1 **a** h = 16 cm; w = 10 cm
b d = 8 cm

2 **a** l = 5 metres; w = 4 metres
b 18 metres

3 **a** 30 metres
b

$$\begin{array}{r} 22 \\ 55 \\ 30 \\ +\ 42 \\ \hline 149 \text{ metres} \end{array}$$

4 **b** 6.8 metres
c 34 m^2

5 BC = 5.5 km

6 **a** 9.1 metres
b 6 cars

7 **a** 5.3 miles
b

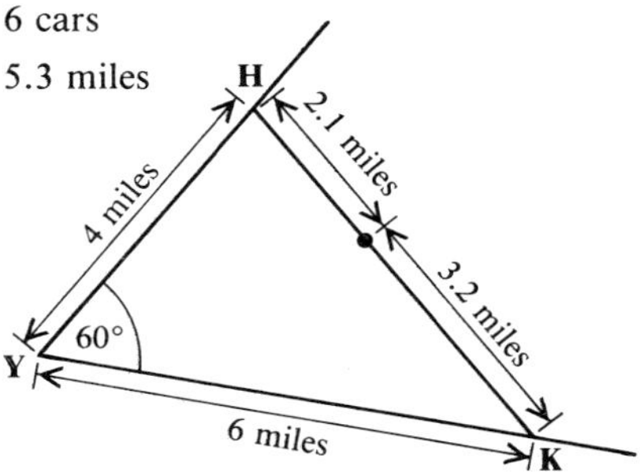

Scale drawings and loci

8 **b** $XY = 7.5$ metres

9 **a** 6 m

b 8 m

10 **b** 30 m

11

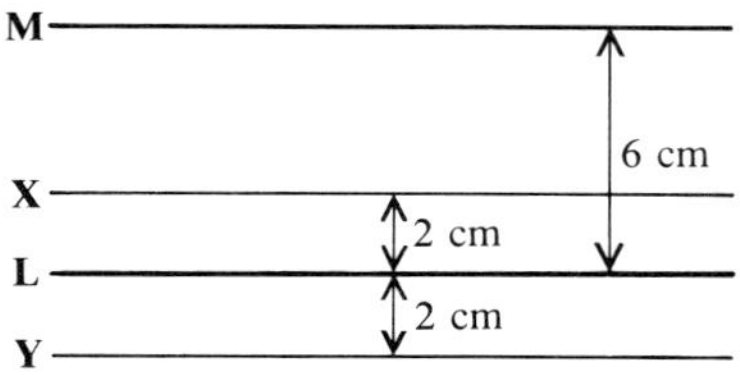

12

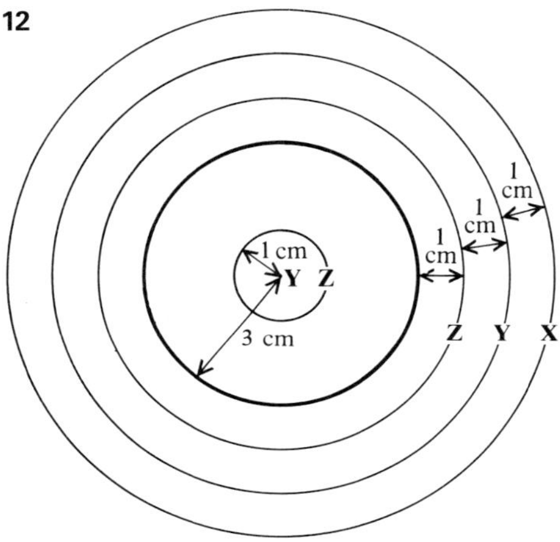

13

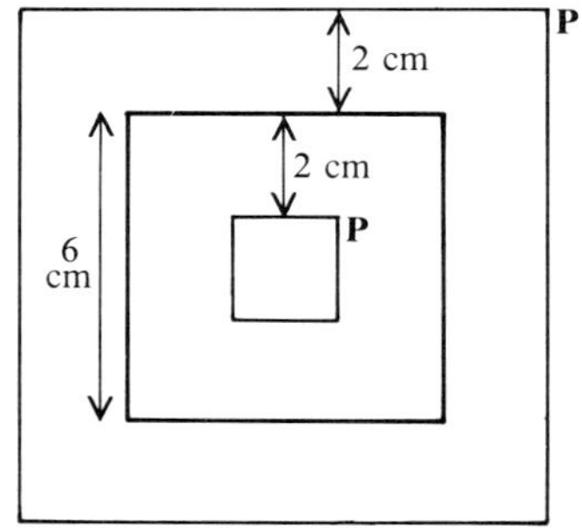

14

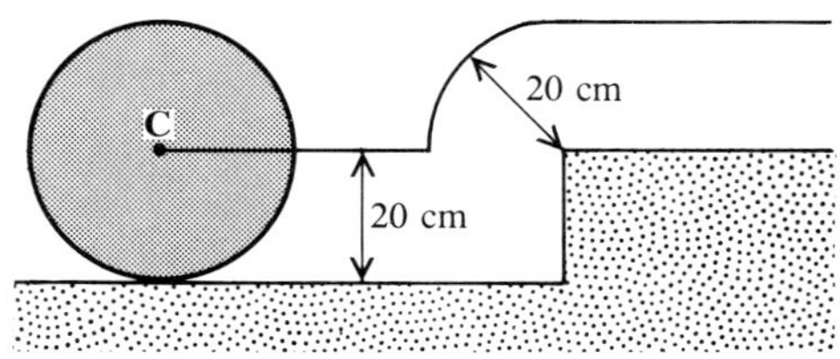

15

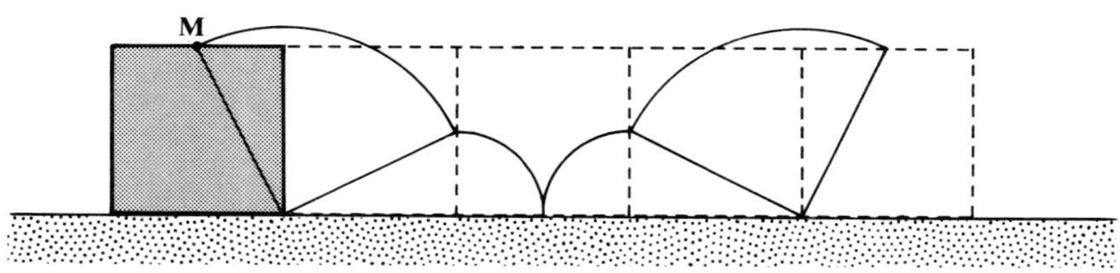

16 **a**

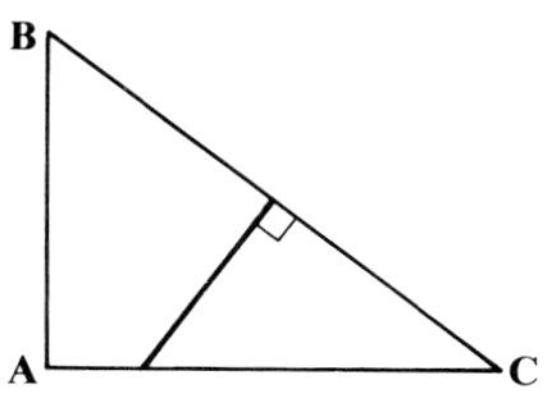

b

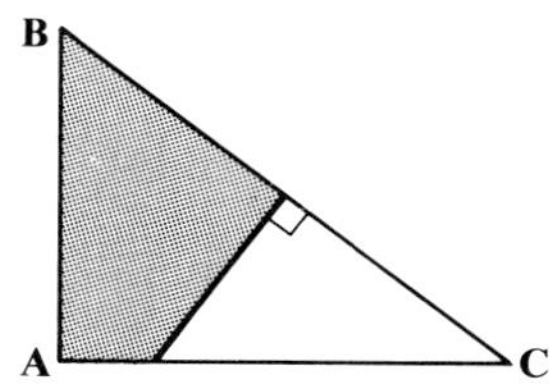

c

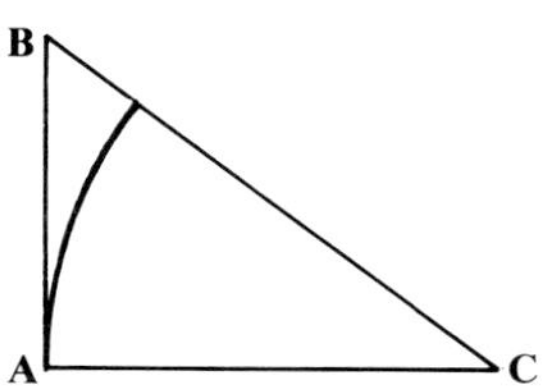

d

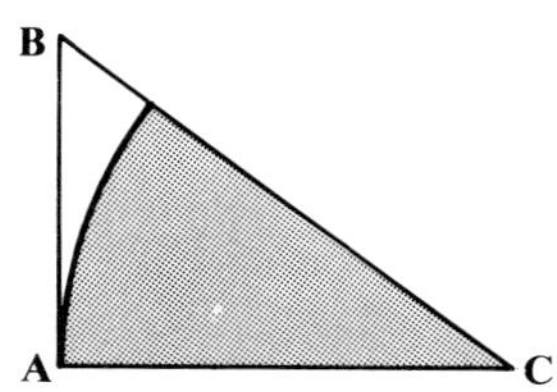

Scale drawings and loci

17 **a**

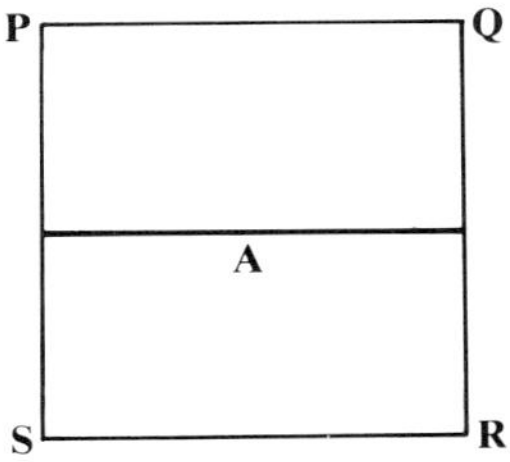

b

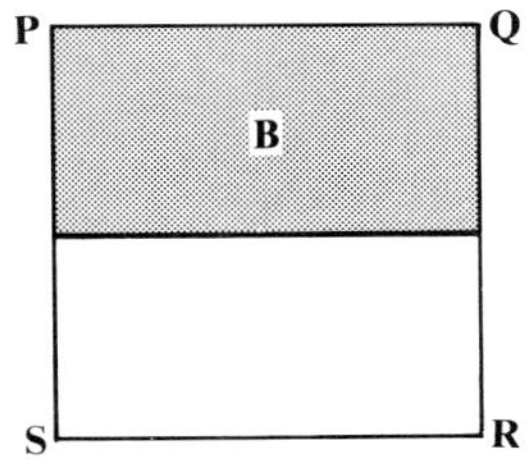

c

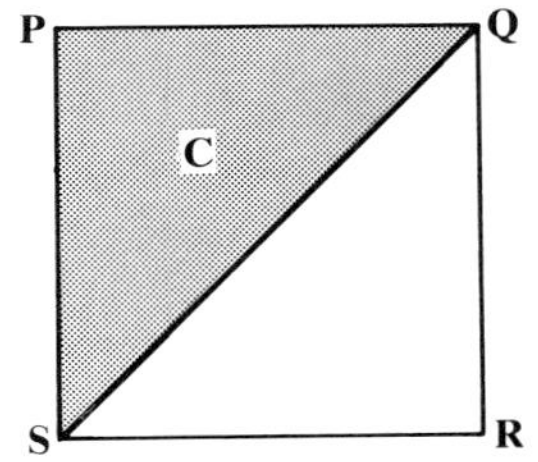

Trigonometry

Part 1 Pythagoras' Theorem

1 **a** 5.54 cm **b** 8.32 cm **c** 7.03 cm **d** 7.66 cm
2 7.08 km
3 7.32 cm
4 **a** 8.35 cm **b** 11.8 m
5 **a** (i) 5 cm (ii) 13 cm **b** (i) 7.21 cm (ii) 8.77 cm
6 **a** 1.84 m
b 2.44 m

Part 2 Sine, cosine and tangent

Sine of an angle

1 **a** 48.6° **b** 41.8° **c** 59.3° **d** 13.3°
2 **a** 2.65 cm **b** 4.17 cm **c** 11.8 cm **d** 2.61 cm
3 20°
4 8.74 cm
5 38.7°

Cosine of an angle

6 **a** 51.3° **b** 33.6° **c** 42.3° **d** 48.2°
7 **a** 2.65 cm **b** 5.56 cm **c** 21.0 cm **d** 0.965 cm
8 14.8°
9 1.64 m
10 20°

Tangent of an angle

11 **a** 33.7° **b** 36.9° **c** 51.3° **d** 53.1°
12 **a** 6.4 cm **b** 21.6 cm **c** 4.14 cm **d** 9.86 cm
13 58.0°
14 150 m
15 35.0°

A mixture

16 059°
17 23.6°
18 11.8 cm
19 522 m
20 36.9°
21 66.0°
22 39°
23 **a** 45°
b 3.83 cm

Trigonometry

Part 3 The right-angled triangle

1 49.4°
2 25.4°
3 59.7°
4 5.22 km
5 9.22 units
6 1.61 m
7 32 m
8 14 m
9 a 72 m
b 31°

10 a 1.5 km
b 0.89 km
c 30.7°

11 a 163 metres
b 147 metres
c 42°

12 a 19 cm
b 11.2 cm
c 7.8 cm

Part 4 Latitude and longitude

1 a 60°N, 10°E b 20°N, 80°W c 30°N, 120°E
d 0°, 30°E e 35°S, 70°W f 20°S, 35°E
g 35°S, 150°E h 80°S, 50°W i 40°S, 175°E
j 40°N, 105°W k 25°N, 85°E l 20°S, 180°

2 a 40°S, 175°E
b 37°N, 3°W
c 32°S, 115°E
d 36°N, 125°E

3 a along the meridian 3°E
b along the Equator
c over the North Pole
d over the North Pole

4 a 1780 km
b 5670 km
c 556 km
d 16700 km
e 7670 km

5 1440 km; 1655 GMT

Symmetry

Part 1 Two dimensions

1 a
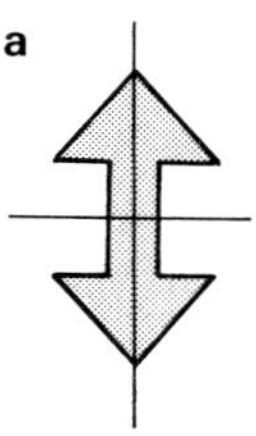
b
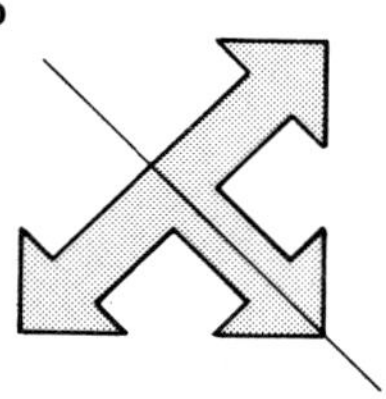
c
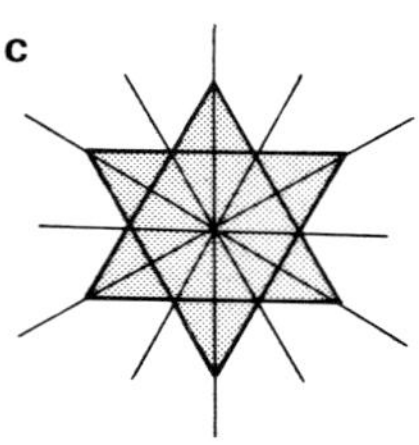
d
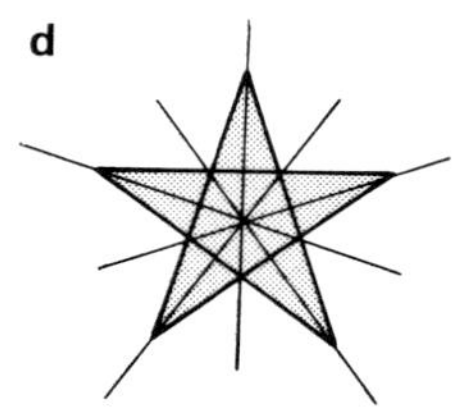

2 a two b four c none
d two e one f none (unless it is isosceles in which case, one)

3 a
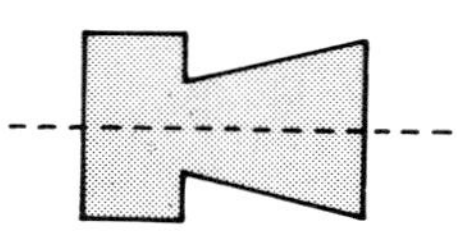
b
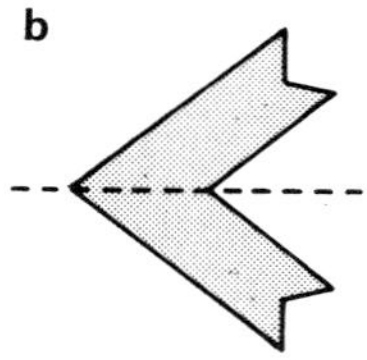
c
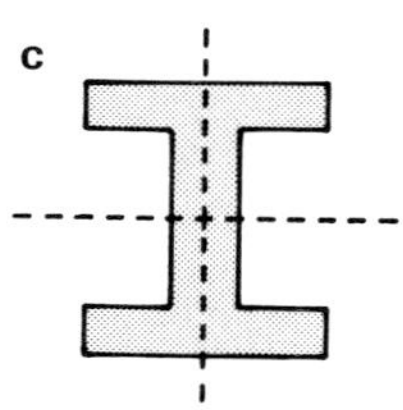
d
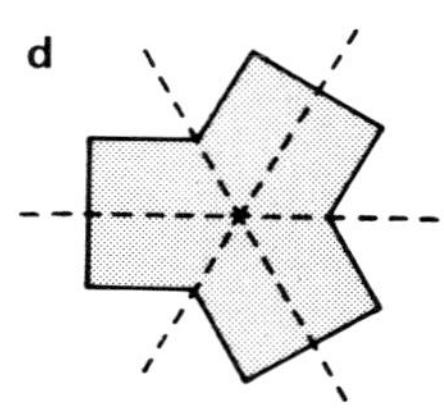

4 a order 3 b order 5 c none d order 4

5 a order 2 b none c order 6 d order 5

Symmetry

6 **a**

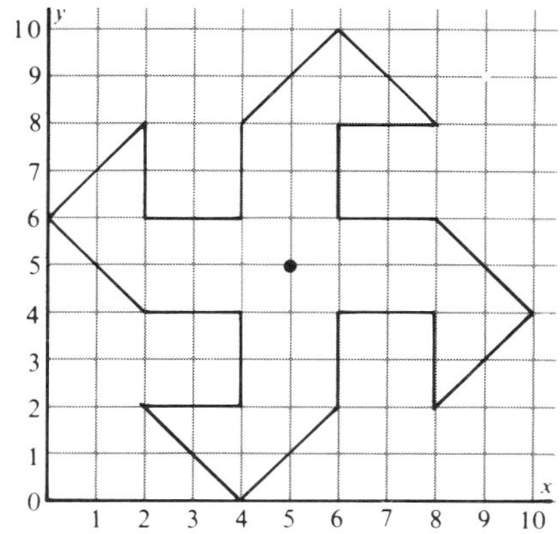

b

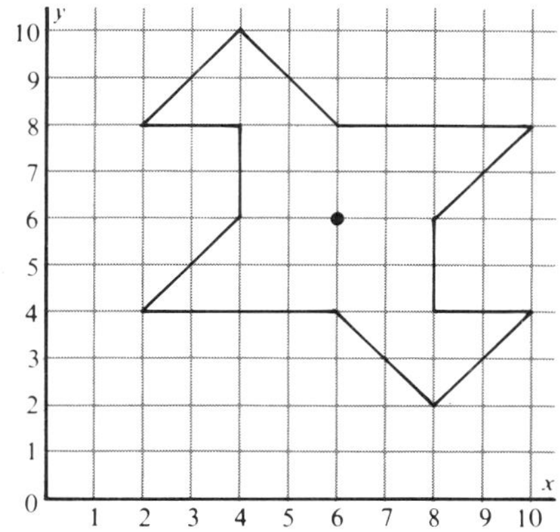

c

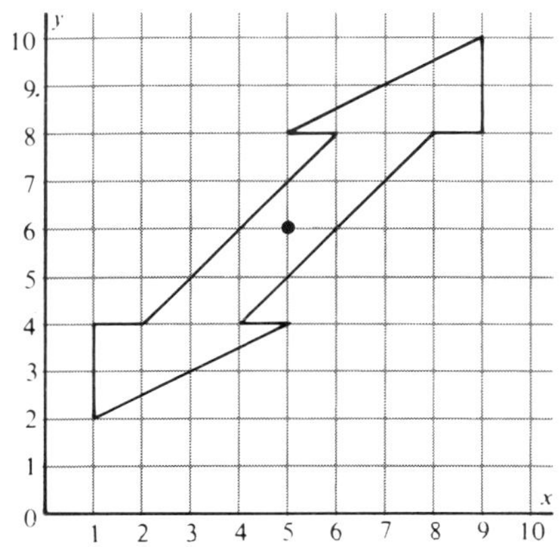

7

	8♦	oxo	noon
a	none	2	1
b	order 2	order 2	none

8

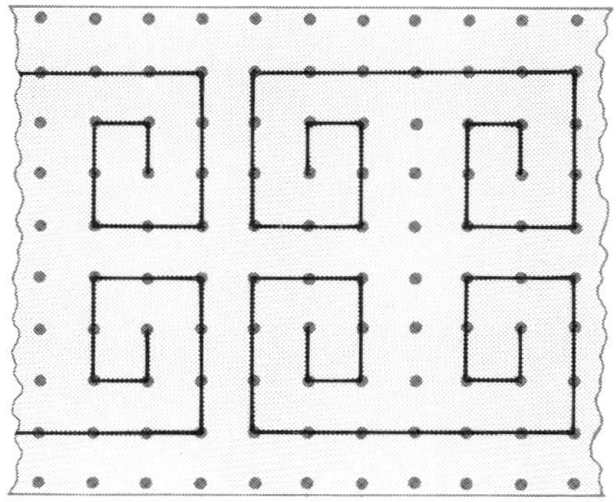

9

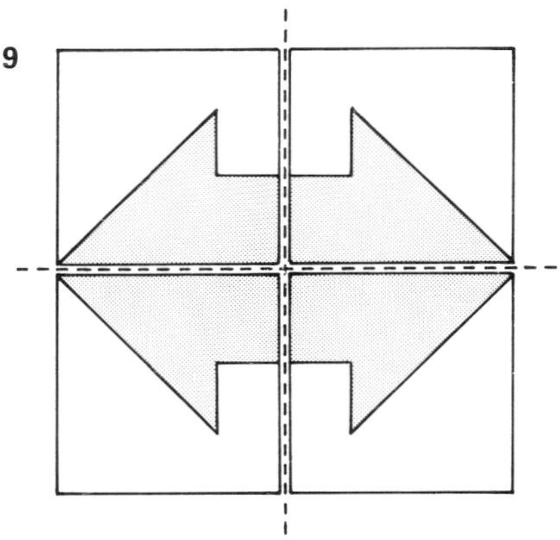

Part 2 Three dimensions

1 **a** order 4 **b** order 2 **c** order 5 **d** order 2

2 **a, c, d**

3 **a, b, c**

4 **b, d**

5 **a** 1 **b** 1 **c** 7
d 2 **e** 2 **f** 9

Transformations

Part 1 Reflections

1 I, U

2 five past five

3 **a**

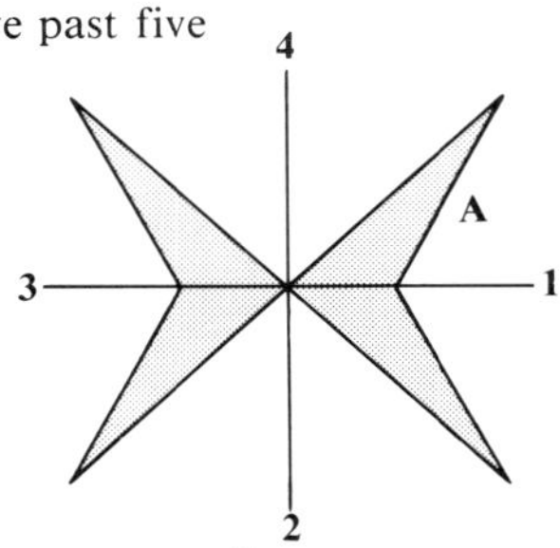

b

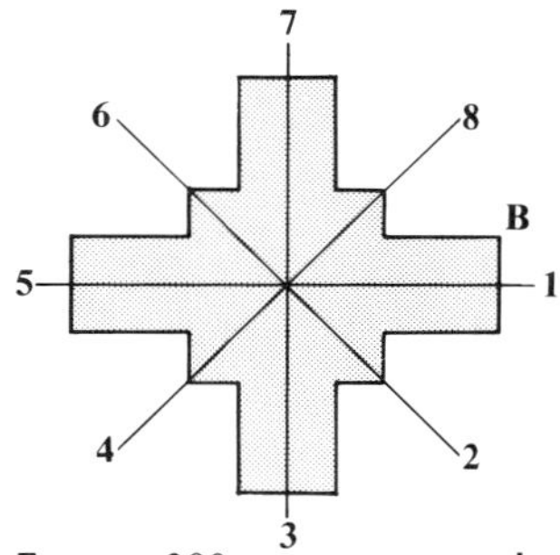

4

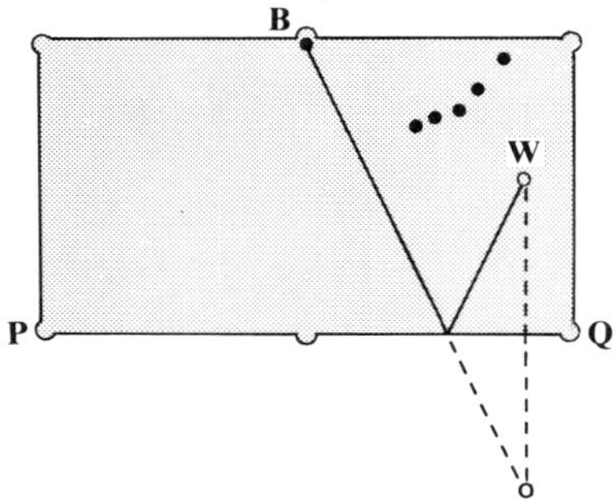

5 **a** 30° **b** 60°
c 30° **d** 60°

6 **a** 45° **b** 65°
c 130° **d** 70°
e 140°

7 **a** 40° **b** 80°
c 50° **d** 100°

8 **a** 70° **b** 20°
c 50° **d** 95°

9 **a** 70° **b** 20°
c 50° **d** 40°

10 **a**

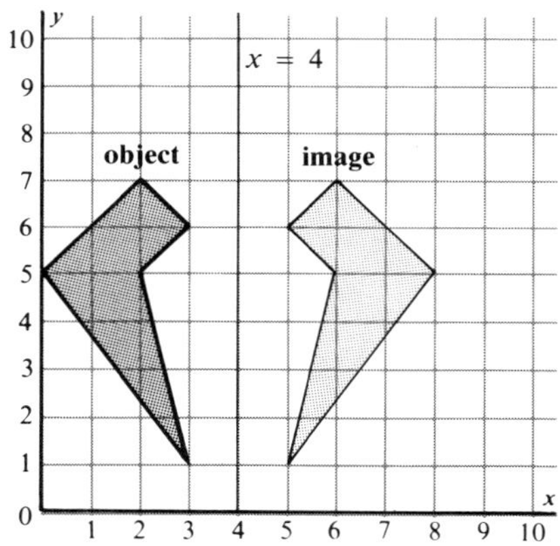

b

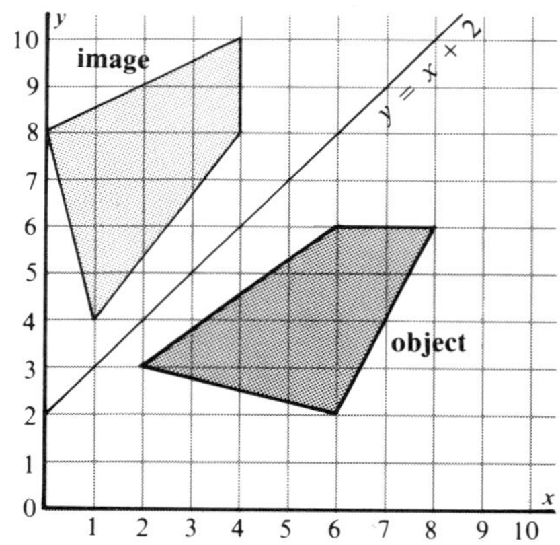

c

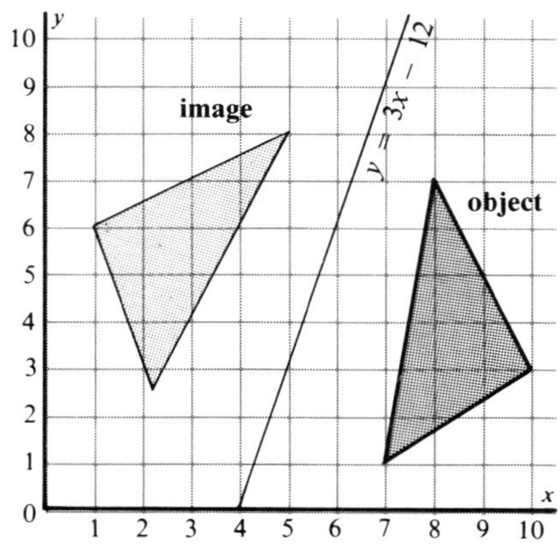

Transformations

11 **a**

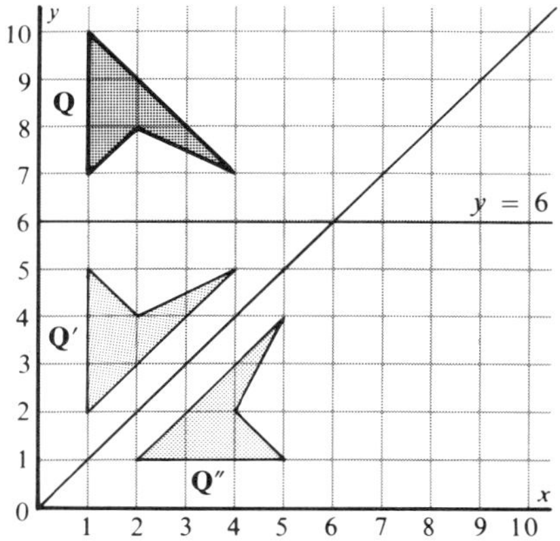

b An anticlockwise quarter turn about the point (6, 6).

13

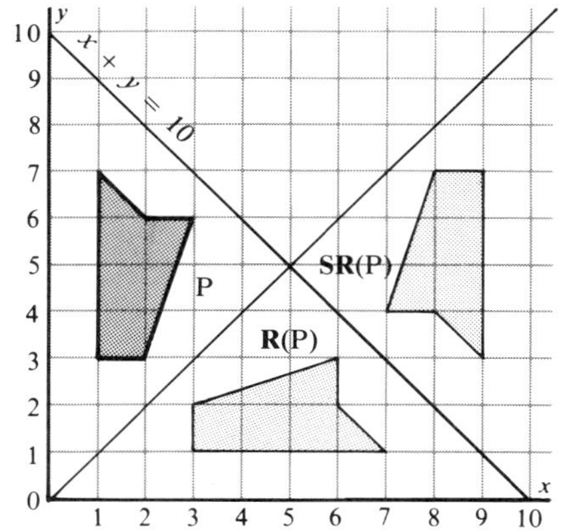

A half turn about the point (5, 5).

12

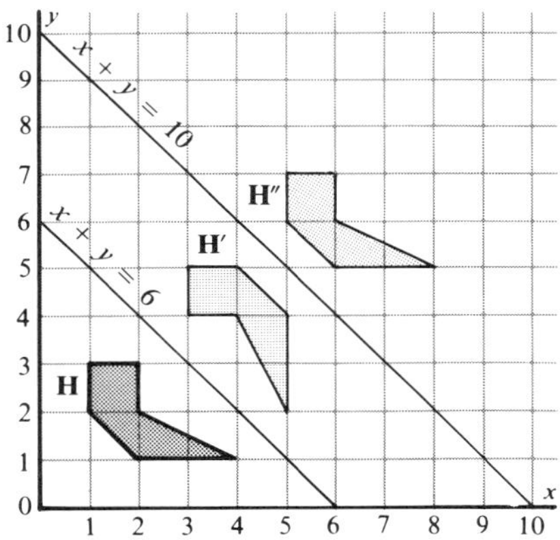

A translation of $\begin{pmatrix} 4 \\ 4 \end{pmatrix}$.

14

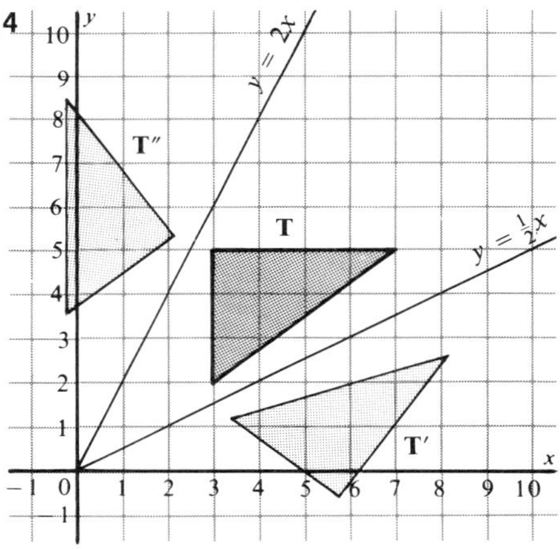

Part 2 Rotations

1 **a** a half turn **b** three-quarters of a full turn **c** a quarter-turn

2 **a** 60° clockwise
b 120° clockwise
c 240° clockwise

3 **c**

4 **b** The triangle rotates through 73°.
The rectangle rotates through 58°.
c *B* moves 12.7 cm
X moves 5.06 cm

5 **a** 30° **b** 30°
c 30°
d 120°

6 **a** 50° **b** 40°
c 50°

7 **a** 75° **b** 75°
c 75°
d 30°

8 **a** 90° anticlockwise about (6, 7)
b 180° about (6, 6)
c 90° clockwise about (5, 4)

9 **a** centre *C* (1, 2)
angle of rotation 45° anticlockwise
$CQ = 6$ units; arc $QQ' = 4.7$ units
b centre *C* (3, 7)
angle of rotation 90° anticlockwise
arc $ZZ' = 8$ units
c centre *C* (6, 3)
angle of rotation 90° clockwise
$CM = 5$ units; arc $MM' = 7.85$ units

Transformations

10 a

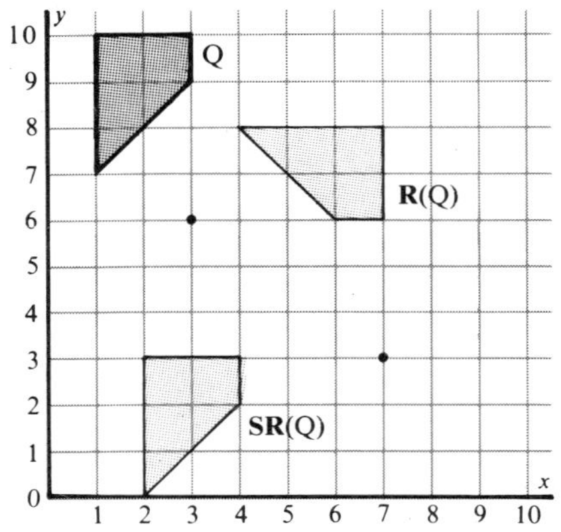

b A translation of $\begin{pmatrix} 1 \\ -7 \end{pmatrix}$.

11 a

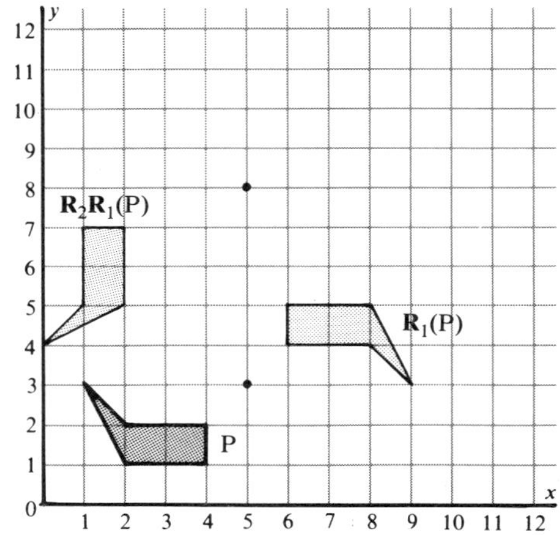

b An anticlockwise rotation of 90° about the point (0, 3).

Part 3 Vectors and translations

1 vector: **a, d** scalar: **b, c**

2

Vector	Magnitude km	Direction (bearing)
p	2	040°
q	3	090°
r	1.5	070°
s	2.5	150°
t	4	055°
u	2.5	200°

3 $\mathbf{a} = \begin{pmatrix} 1 \\ 3 \end{pmatrix}$ $\mathbf{b} = \begin{pmatrix} 5 \\ 2 \end{pmatrix}$ $\mathbf{c} = \begin{pmatrix} 2 \\ -3 \end{pmatrix}$

$\mathbf{d} = \begin{pmatrix} 5 \\ 0 \end{pmatrix}$ $\mathbf{e} = \begin{pmatrix} -1 \\ 2 \end{pmatrix}$ $\mathbf{f} = \begin{pmatrix} 5 \\ 1 \end{pmatrix}$

$\mathbf{g} = \begin{pmatrix} -1 \\ -5 \end{pmatrix}$

4 a $\mathbf{r} = \begin{pmatrix} 10 \\ 3 \end{pmatrix}$
b no

5 $\mathbf{r} = \begin{pmatrix} 5 \\ -3 \end{pmatrix}$

6 10 units of force

7 a 1.5 units of force **b** zero

8 a 410 km/h on a bearing of 027° **b** 205 km/h due north

9 $\mathbf{x} = \mathbf{a} + \mathbf{b}$
$\mathbf{y} = \mathbf{a} + \mathbf{b} + \mathbf{c}$
$\mathbf{z} = \mathbf{a} + \mathbf{b} + \mathbf{c} + \mathbf{d}$

10 a $3\mathbf{p}$ **b** $2\mathbf{q}$ **c** $-\mathbf{q}$ **d** $-2\mathbf{p}$
e $-\mathbf{p}$ **f** $-2\mathbf{q}$ **g** $-\mathbf{q}$ **h** $\mathbf{p} - \mathbf{q}$
i $2\mathbf{p} - 2\mathbf{q}$ **j** $3\mathbf{p} - 3\mathbf{q}$

11 a $\mathbf{a}$ **b** $\mathbf{b}$ **c** $\mathbf{a}$ **d** $2\mathbf{a}$
e $3\mathbf{a}$ **f** $\mathbf{a} + \mathbf{b}$ **g** $2(\mathbf{a} + \mathbf{b})$ **h** $3(\mathbf{a} + \mathbf{b})$
i $\mathbf{a} + \mathbf{b}$ **j** $3(\mathbf{a} + \mathbf{b})$

12 $\mathbf{MN} = \mathbf{p} + \mathbf{q}$
$\mathbf{AB} = 2(\mathbf{p} + \mathbf{q})$
AB is parallel to and twice the length of MN

13 a $\mathbf{u} + \mathbf{v}$ **b** $\mathbf{v}$ **c** $\mathbf{u}$ **d** $\mathbf{u} + \mathbf{v}$
AP is parallel to and equal in length to QC.

Transformations

14

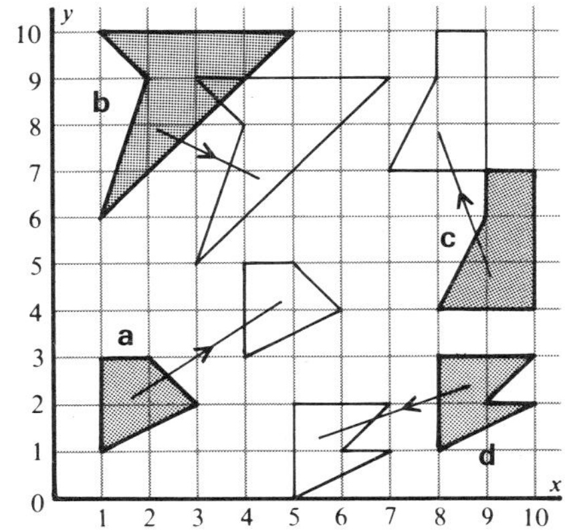

a $\begin{pmatrix} 3 \\ 2 \end{pmatrix}$ **b** $\begin{pmatrix} 2 \\ -1 \end{pmatrix}$

c $\begin{pmatrix} -1 \\ 3 \end{pmatrix}$ **d** $\begin{pmatrix} -3 \\ -1 \end{pmatrix}$

15 **b** A translation given by the vector $\begin{pmatrix} 6 \\ -2 \end{pmatrix}$.

16 **a** (i) true
(ii) true
(iii) false
(iv) true
(v) false
(vi) true

b

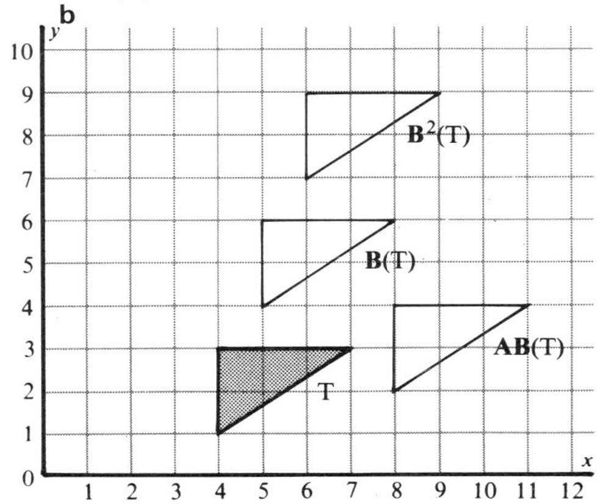

Part 4 Stretches

1 **a** stretch **b** enlargement **c** neither
d enlargement **e** stretch **f** stretch

2 object 1: scale factor 2 object 2: scale factor 3

3

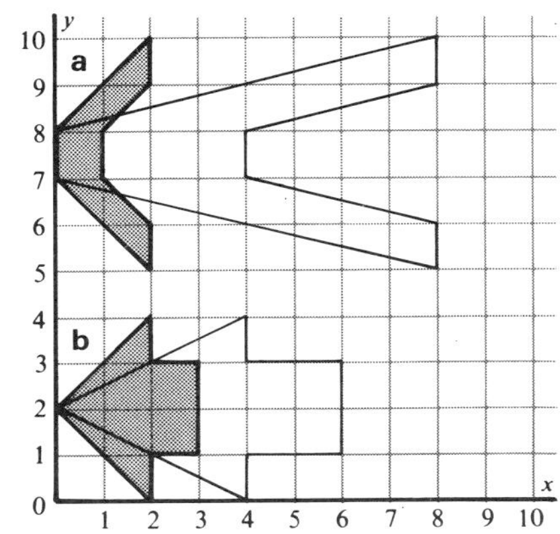

a 4 **b** 2

4

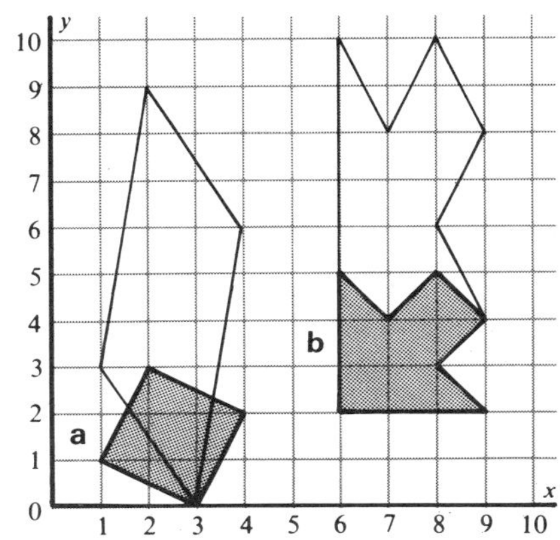

Transformations

5

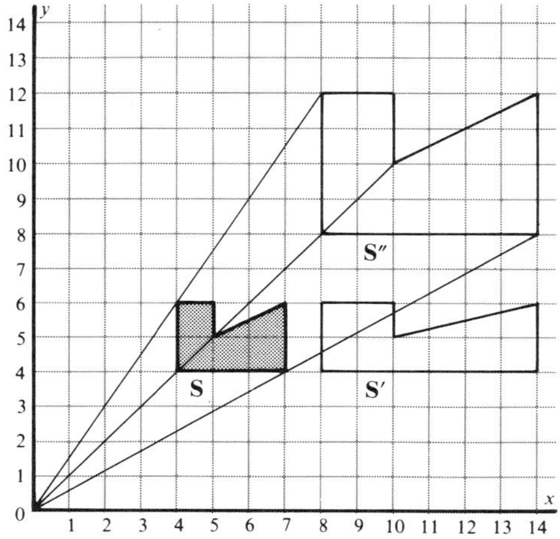

An enlargement, centre the origin and length scale factor 2.

Part 5 Enlargements

1 20

2 **a** 3
b 9

3 **a**

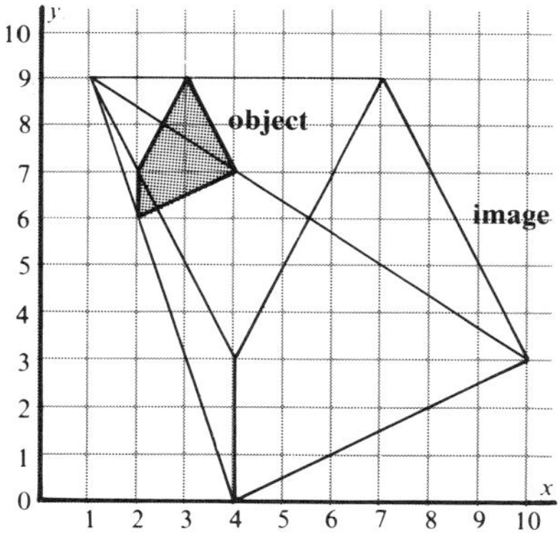

(i) (1, 9) (ii) 3 (iii) 9

b

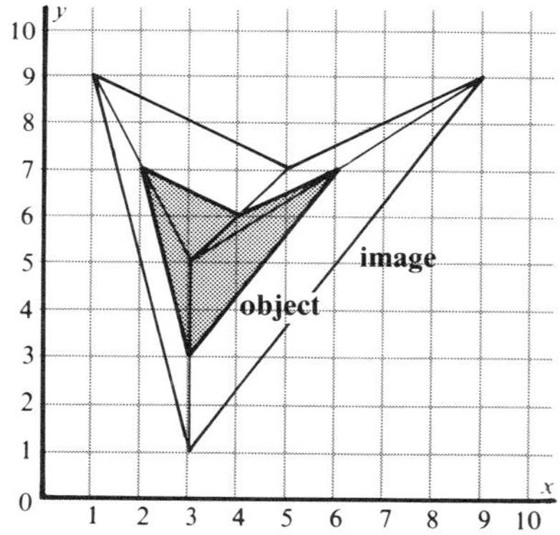

(i) (3, 5) (ii) 2 (iii) 4

c

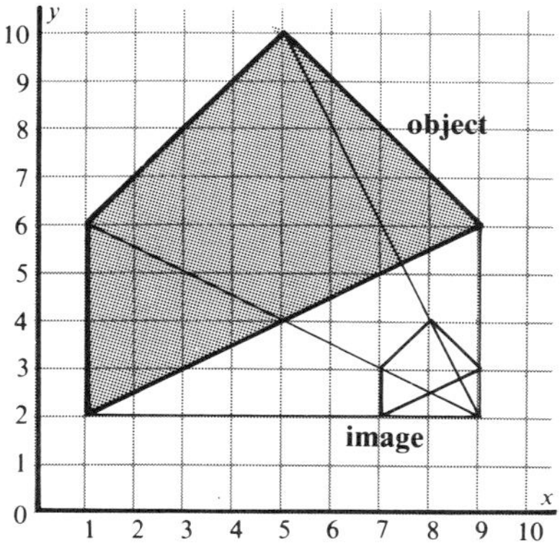

(i) (9, 2) (ii) $\frac{1}{4}$ (iii) $\frac{1}{16}$

d

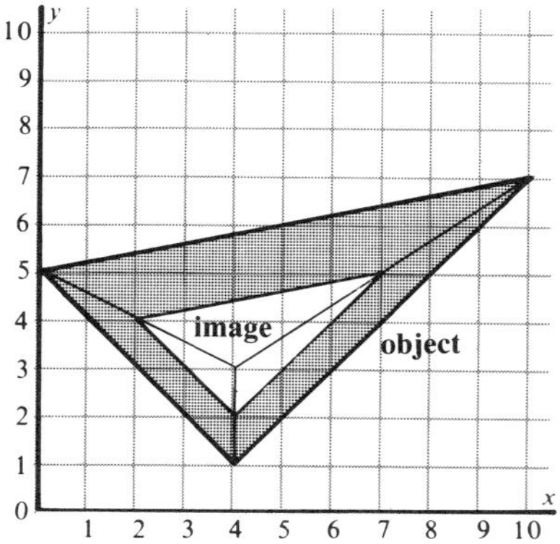

(i) (4, 3) (ii) $\frac{1}{2}$ (iii) $\frac{1}{4}$

Transformations

e

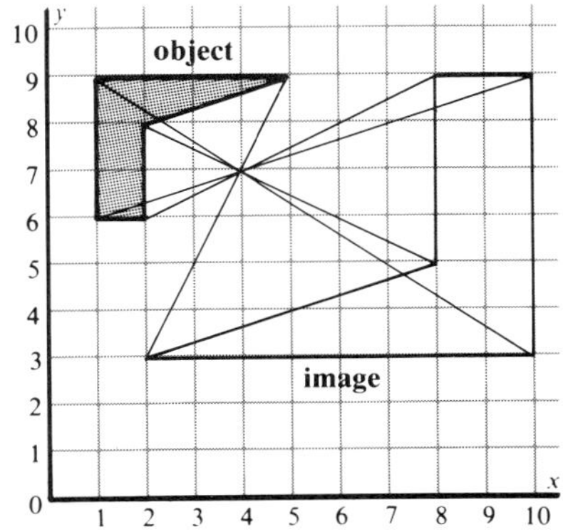

(i) (4, 7) (ii) −2 (iii) 4

4 **a**

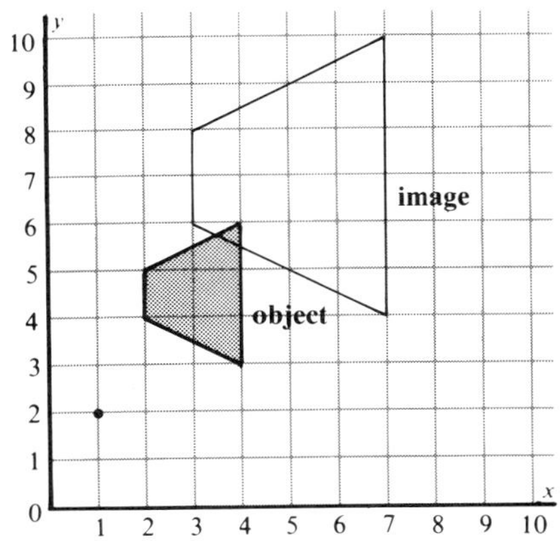

b

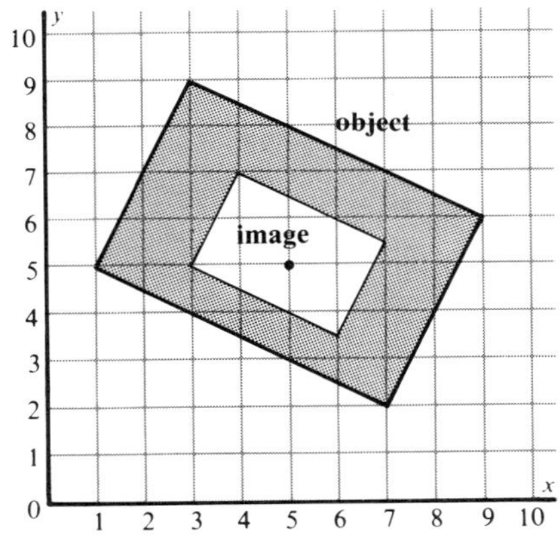

c

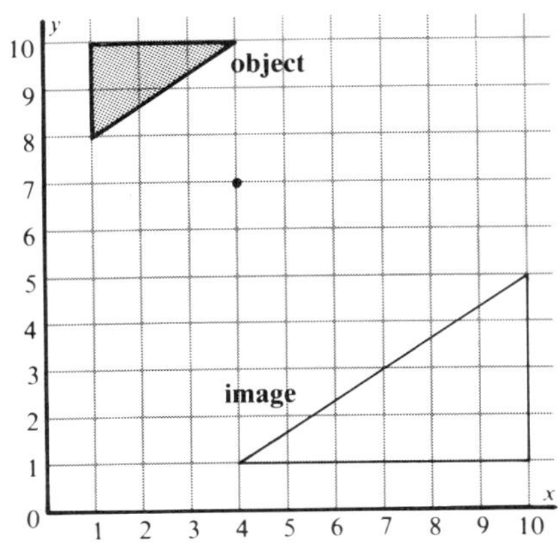

Transformations

5

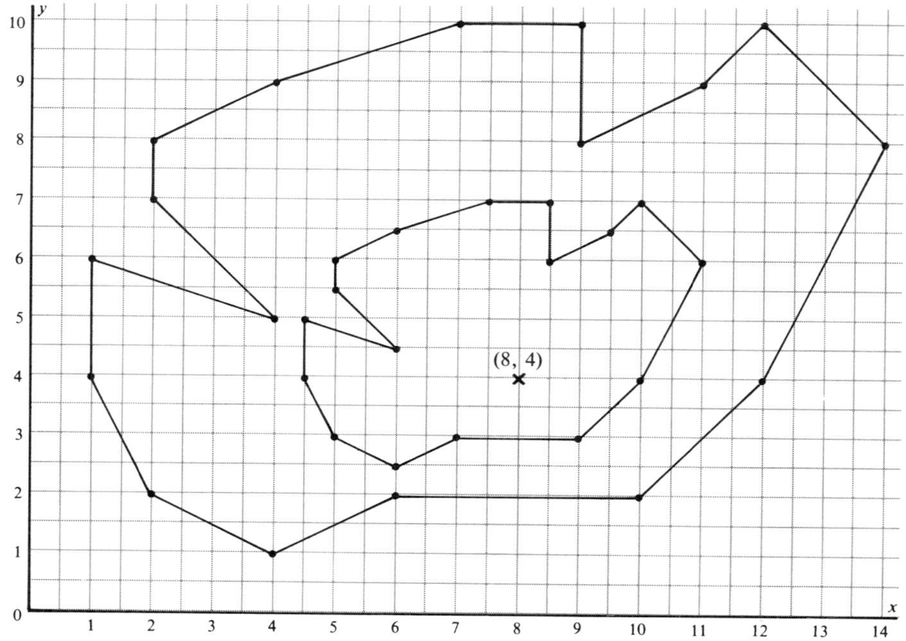

6 a

	Map A	Map B
Length of rail track, cm	3	6
Shortest distance from PO to church, cm	$2\frac{1}{2}$	5
Area of wood, cm^2	1	4

b 2
c 4

7 a 12 cm
b 9
c 54 cm^2
d 48 cm^2

8 a 4
b 16
c 8 cm
d 40 cm^2
e $37\frac{1}{2}$ cm^2

9 a

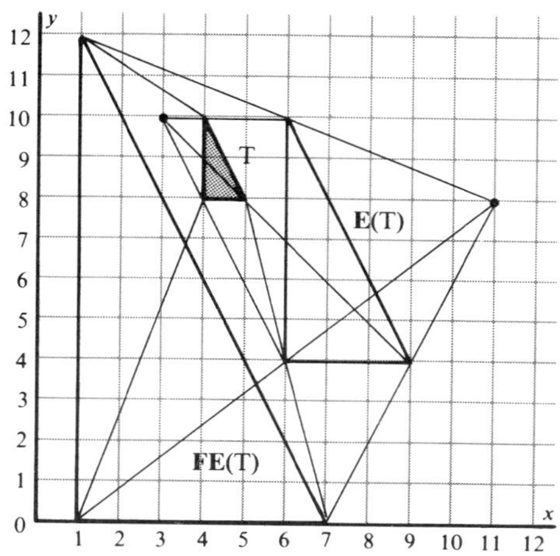

b An enlargement of length scale factor 6 and centre (4.6, 9.6).

10 a

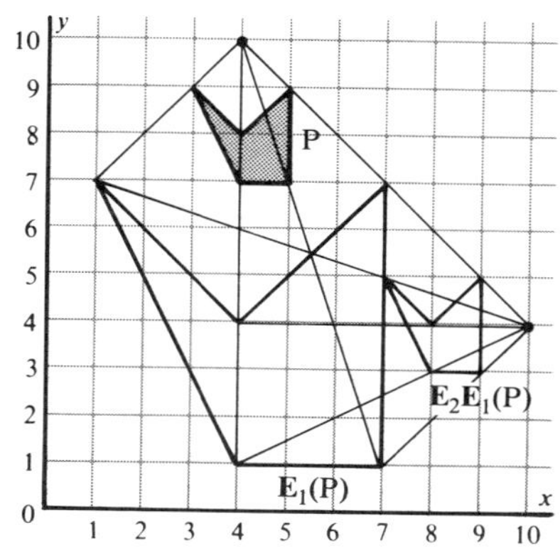

b A translation of $\begin{pmatrix} 4 \\ -4 \end{pmatrix}$

Transformations

Part 6 Similarity

1 **a** similar **b** congruent **c** neither

2 A, F
B, D
C, E

3 **a** congruent
b similar
c congruent
d neither

4

Length scale factor	2	3	4	5	6	7	8	9	10	m
Area scale factor	4	9	16	25	36	49	64	81	100	m^2
Volume scale factor	8	27	64	125	216	343	512	729	1000	m^3

5 **a** 2 **b** 8
c 4 litres

6 **a** 3 **b** 9
c 900 cm^2

7 160 cm^2; 2400 cm^3

8 5 rooms; 1 metre; 1.5 m^2

9 $x = 3$ metres

10 $h = 4\frac{1}{2}$ metres

11 $x = 6$ metres; $y = 9$ metres
15 metres

12 **a** 12 metres; 8 metres
b 24 metres; 6 metres
c 52 metres

13 **a** 3 km **b** 12 km **c** 0.5 km **d** 0.75 km

14 **a** 86 km
b 132 km
c 282 km
d 536 km

15 **a** 2.5 km **b** 5 km **c** 12.5 km **d** 1.25 km **e** 4 km

16 **a** 1:400 000 **b** 1:500 000
c 1:800 000 **d** 1:800 000
e 1:250 000 **f** 1:50 000

17 1:25 000 000

18 20 km; 75 km^2

19 32 km; 400 km^2

20 1:50 000

Topology

1 A, F B, H C, D E, G

2 b

3 **a**

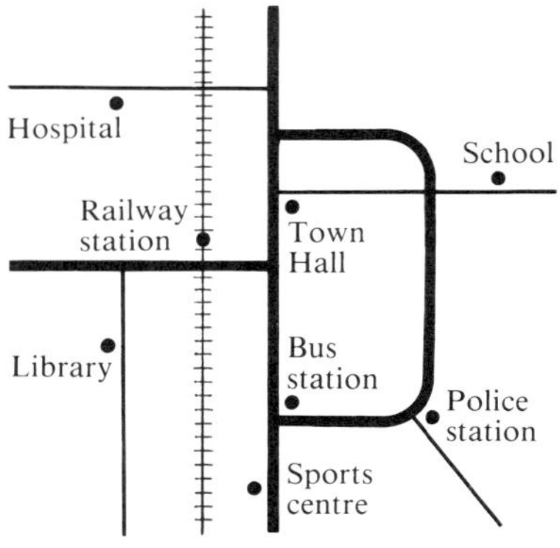

b Turn right out of the school gates, right at the main road, right at the T-junction, first left, cross the railway bridge and the hospital is on your left.

c Turn left out of the railway station, right at the T-junction, first left after the bus station and the police station is on your right.

Topology

4 **a**

A	Leeds	*B*	Harrogate
C	York	*D*	Selby
E	Doncaster	*F*	Ilkley
G	Skipton	*H*	Keighley
I	Bradford (Forster Square)	*J*	Bradford (Interchange)
K	Halifax	*L*	Rochdale
M	Manchester (Victoria)	*N*	Stalybridge
O	Huddersfield	*P*	Dewsbury
Q	Wakefield (Westgate)	*R*	Wakefield (Kirkgate)
S	Castleford	*T*	Pontefract Baghill
U	Barnsley	*V*	Penistone
W	Sheffield	*X*	Rotherham
Y	Todmorden	*Z*	Knaresborough

b **1** Newcastle
2 Lancaster
3 London
4 Goole
5 Hull

c (i) Map 1
(ii) Map 2

d Distances have been distorted.

5 *sphere:*
a golfball, a screw,
a hat, a pair of tweezers,
a potato

torus:
a wedding ring, a cup,
a saw

double torus:
a pair of scissors,
a cardigan,
swimming trunks,
a kettle

6 **a** no odd nodes
b 2 odd nodes
c 4 odd nodes
d 4 odd nodes

a and **b** are traversable.

7 Yes; Motherwell and Perth.

8 **a** no
b yes

9

to

$$\begin{array}{c} \\ B \\ C \\ H \\ L \end{array} \begin{array}{c} \begin{array}{cccc} B & C & H & L \end{array} \\ \begin{pmatrix} 0 & 2 & 0 & 2 \\ 2 & 0 & 2 & 1 \\ 0 & 2 & 0 & 1 \\ 2 & 1 & 1 & 0 \end{pmatrix} \end{array}$$

10 **a**

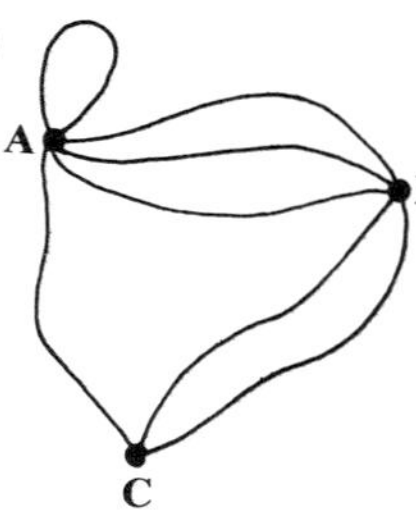

b

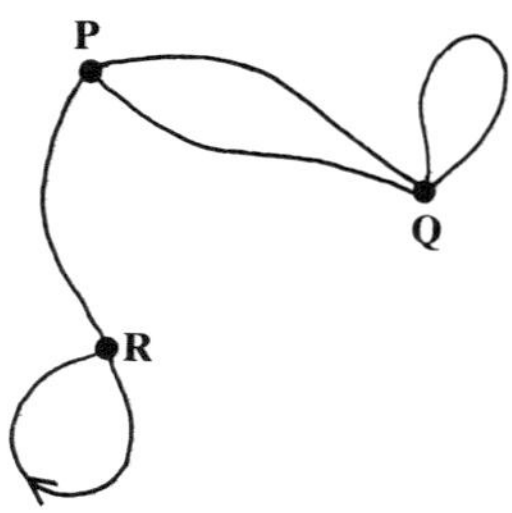

c

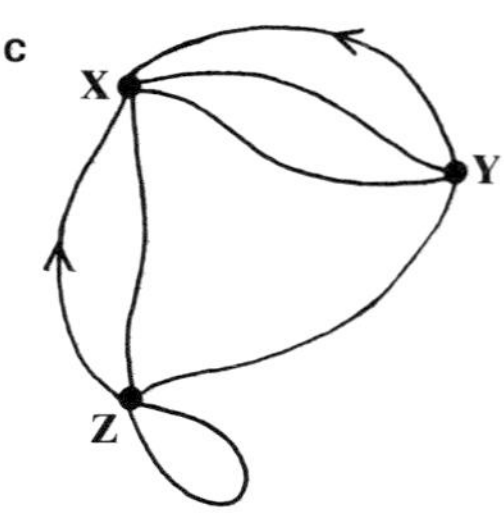

Tables, charts and matrices

Part 1 Tabulation of information

1 **a** Menston plc of Coventry
b £35
c £144
d 150 m
e 3rd April 1986

f

	£
Total before VAT	805·00
VAT at 15%	120·75
TOTAL AMOUNT DUE	925·75
5% discount	46·29
Net cost after discount	879·46

Tables, charts and matrices

2 **a** 07.07
b 07.45
c 08.50
d 09.45; 33 minutes
e the *340* service; 10.21
f 13.37 (or 1.37 p.m.)
g 22.21
h 23.45; 00.05; 20 minutes

3 **a** (i) 34p
(ii) 45p
(iii) 30p
(iv) 30p
b £1·34
c £1·50

4 **a** £15
b (i) £156
(ii) £8
c £310

5 **a** 12p
b 81p
c £1·15
d 81p
e 6p
f 17p; 0943-4308
g 12 units; 69p
h 36 units; £2·07

6 **a** £57·33
b £96·37
c £166·29
d (i) £67·68; 3.1 m^2
(ii) £75·98; 3.28 m^2
£21·83 per m^2 and £23·16 gives (i) as the 'better buy'.
e The average of the quoted prices is £64·07

7 **a** £67·50
b 4 m × 6 m; £72·60; polypropylene
c £50·00 for cash
£55·00 over 20 weeks
£5 is saved
d Over 20 weeks: £84·00
Over 38 weeks: £87·78
Cheaper by £3·78 to buy over 20 weeks
e SG 023 £3·54 per m^2
SG 035 £3·21 per m^2
The larger carpet is *relatively* cheaper.
f One 4 m × 6 m and one 3 m × 4 m carpet provides the cheapest combination, costing a total of £122·49.
This diagram gives one possible dissection:

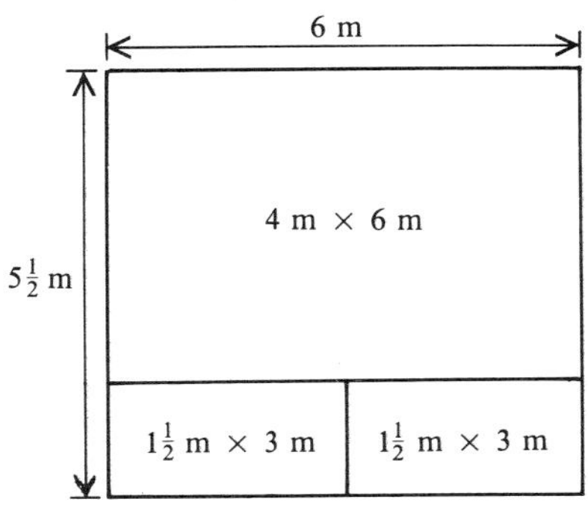

8 **a** £79·99, reduced by £10
b Toshiba RT7025R, reduced by £20
c £329·99, reduced by £20
d Sharp VC651, Panasonic NVG10B, Panasonic NVG7B, Samsung V1510T
e (i) Toshiba V66 video recorder, reduced by £80
(ii) Toshiba RT7025R stereo radio cassette, reduced by 22.2%

Tables, charts and matrices

9

Year	1984	1985	1986
British	60	40	30
European	20	30	40
Non-european	30	50	80
Total	110	120	150

10
- **a** 'OK'
- **b** 'OK/fat' borderline
- **c** just over 3 stone
- **d** just over $\frac{1}{2}$ stone
- **e** $10\frac{1}{4}$ to $12\frac{1}{2}$ stone

11

	Canterbury	Dover	Folkestone	Margate	Ramsgate
Canterbury	–	16	17	16	17
Dover	16	–	7	24	20
Folkestone	17	7	–	28	27
Margate	16	24	28	–	4
Ramsgate	17	20	27	4	–

12

Pastry	*Metric*	*Imperial*
Plain flour	270 g	9 oz
Butter	180 g	6 oz
Caster sugar	36 g	$1\frac{1}{2}$ oz
Ground cinnamon	3 teaspn	
Water	3 teaspn	
Egg	1 large yolk	
Filling		
Blackcurrants	720 g	24 oz
Demerara sugar	180 g	6 oz

13

pesetas	1 week	10 days	2 weeks	1 extra week
Espantours	20 000	28 000	36 000	12 000
Iberiaplan	24 000	30 000	35 000	10 000

14

Distance in miles	Railway station	Airport	Police station	Hospital
Rank A	£2·40	£5·60	£2·20	£3·20
Rank B	£2·80	£4·80	£2·40	£2·80

15

	Jan	Feb	Mar	Apr
Electricity	1370	1490	1310	1170
Water	58	56	67	48
Telephone	27	29	26	33

16 $\begin{pmatrix} 24 & 23 \\ 24 & 52 \\ 37 & 35 \end{pmatrix}$ The number of tins and packets of each vegetable sold during the month.

Part 2 Rows and columns

1 $\begin{pmatrix} 27 \end{pmatrix}$

2 $\begin{pmatrix} 4880 \\ 4660 \end{pmatrix}$

3 $\begin{pmatrix} 239 & 223 \\ 163 & 158 \end{pmatrix}$

4
- **a** $\begin{pmatrix} 14 \end{pmatrix}$
- **b** $\begin{pmatrix} 14 \\ 22 \end{pmatrix}$
- **c** $\begin{pmatrix} 14 \\ 22 \\ 18 \end{pmatrix}$
- **d** $\begin{pmatrix} 14 & 20 \\ 22 & 10 \\ 18 & 14 \end{pmatrix}$

5
- **a** $\begin{pmatrix} 8 & 4 \\ 17 & 13 \end{pmatrix}$
- **b** $\begin{pmatrix} 4 & 22 \\ 6 & 8 \end{pmatrix}$
- **c** $\begin{pmatrix} 7 & 9 \\ 15 & 5 \end{pmatrix}$
- **d** $\begin{pmatrix} 8 & 10 & 12 \\ 5 & 7 & 9 \\ 2 & 4 & 6 \end{pmatrix}$
- **e** impossible
- **f** $\begin{pmatrix} 0 & 10 \\ 2 & 6 \\ 4 & 2 \end{pmatrix}$
- **g** $\begin{pmatrix} 18 & 24 & 30 \\ 7 & 11 & 15 \end{pmatrix}$
- **h** impossible

Tables, charts and matrices

Part 3 Transformations

1 a

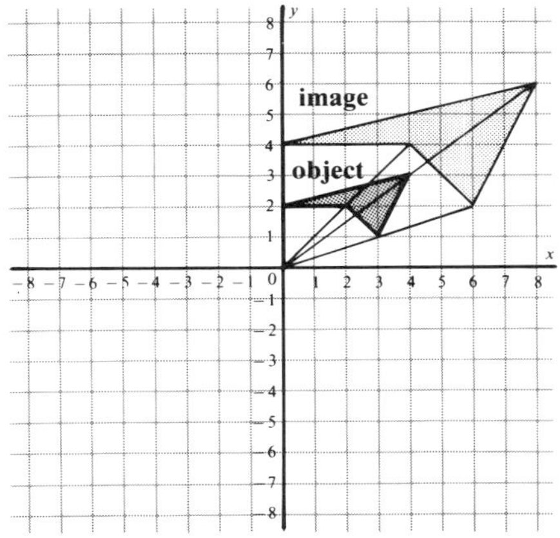

An enlargement, centre the origin and length scale factor 2.

b

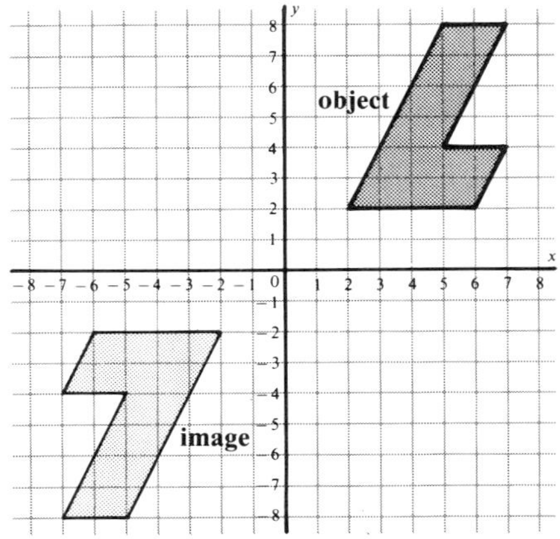

A half-turn rotation about the origin.

c

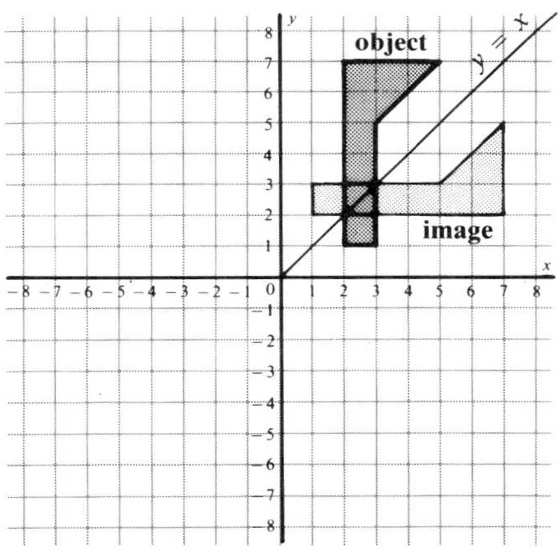

A reflection in the line $y = x$.

d

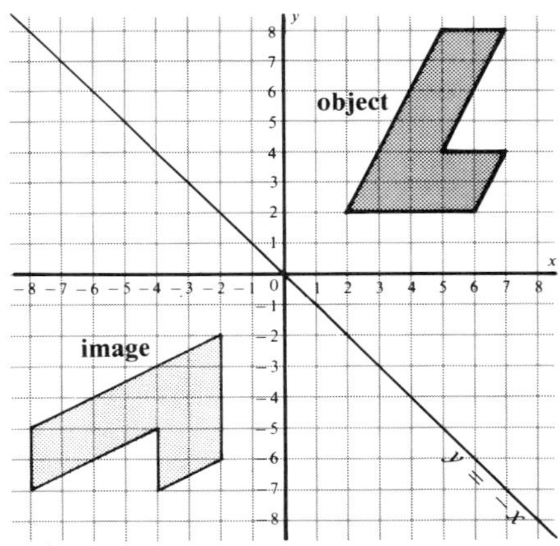

A reflection in the line $y = -x$.

e

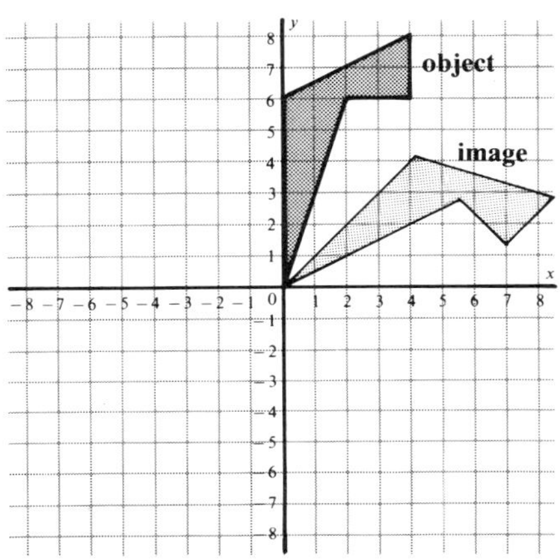

A rotation of 45° clockwise about the origin.

Tables, charts and matrices

2 a

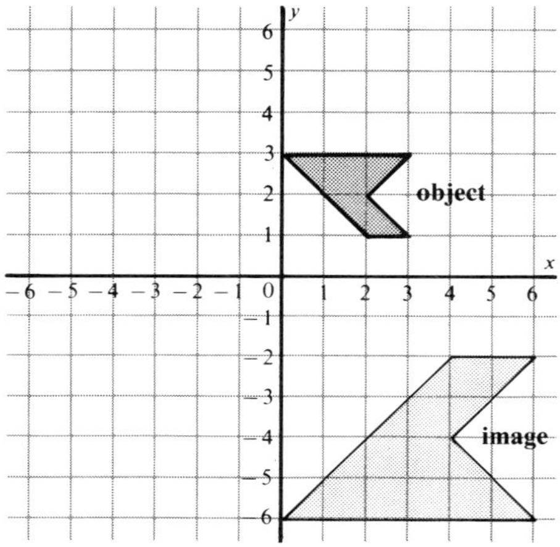

An enlargement of length scale factor 2 (centre the origin) and a reflection in the x-axis.

b

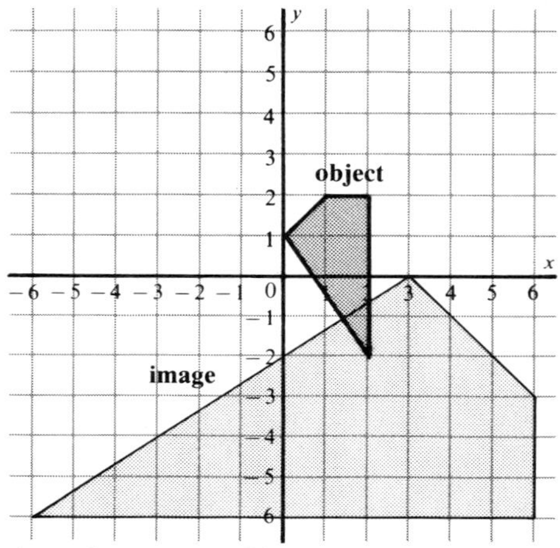

An enlargement of length scale factor 3 (centre the origin), and a clockwise rotation of 90° about the origin.

3

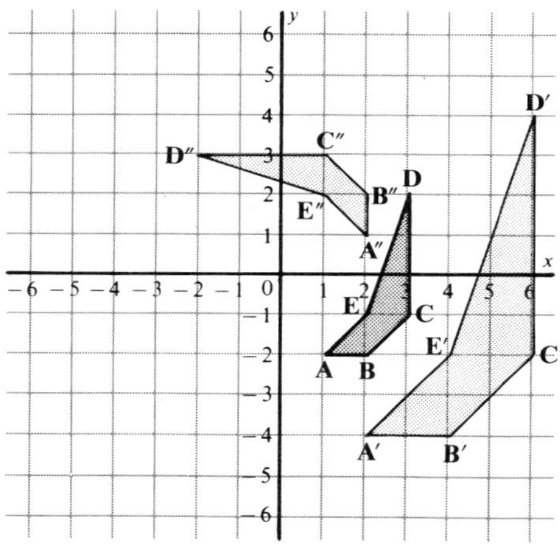

a An enlargement of length scale factor 2 and centre the origin.

c $\begin{pmatrix} 0 & -1 \\ 1 & 0 \end{pmatrix}$ represents an anticlockwise rotation of 90° about the origin.

4

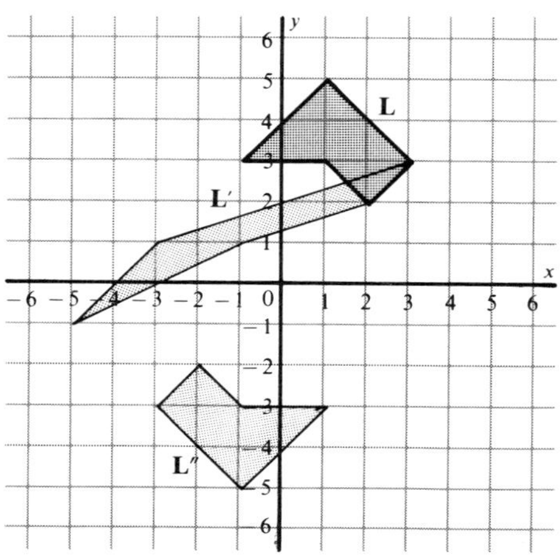

c $\begin{pmatrix} -1 & 0 \\ 0 & -1 \end{pmatrix}$ represents a half-turn about the origin.

Tables, charts and matrices

5

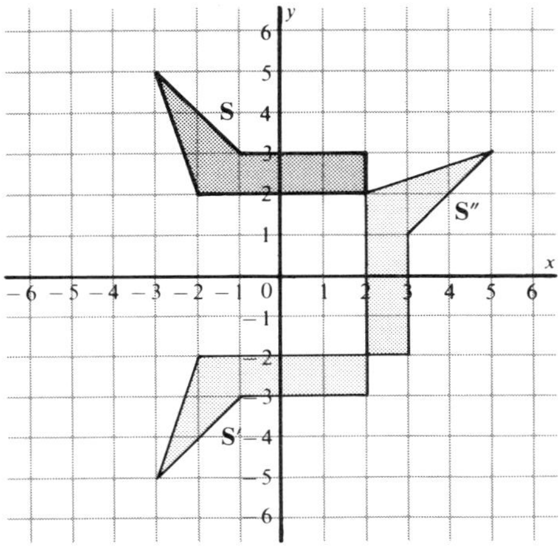

a A reflection in the x-axis.

b A reflection in the line $y = x$.

c $\begin{pmatrix} 0 & 1 \\ -1 & 0 \end{pmatrix}$ represents an anticlockwise rotation of 90° about the origin.

6 **a** 2 **b** 2 **c** 10 **d** 7

7 15 cm^2

8 30 cm^2

Part 4 Inverse matrices

1 **a, b**

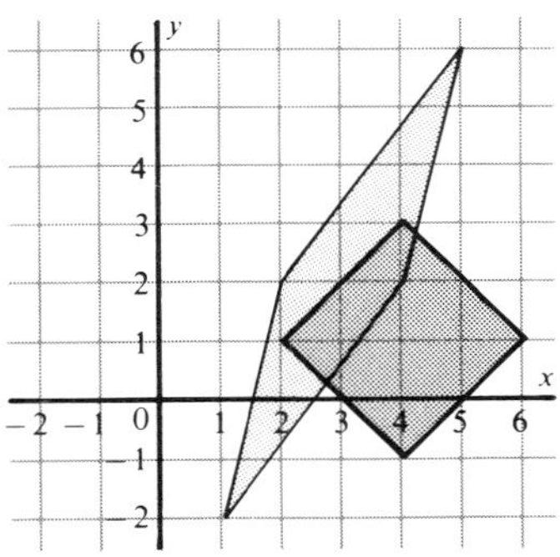

c One is the inverse of the other.

2 **a, b**

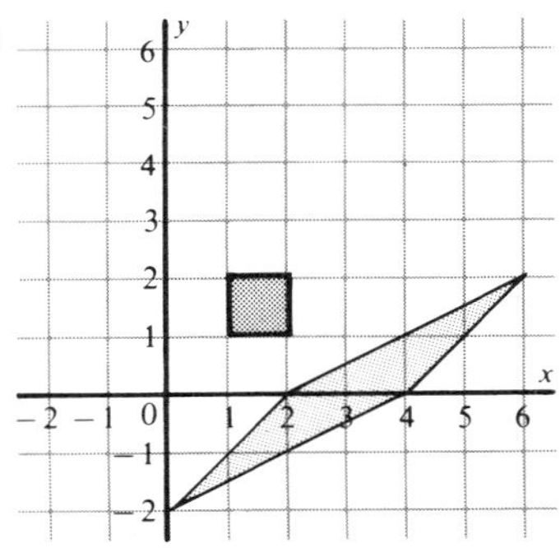

c One is the inverse of the other.

3 **a** (i) 1 (ii) $\begin{pmatrix} 5 & -7 \\ -2 & 3 \end{pmatrix}$

b (i) 2 (ii) $\frac{1}{2}\begin{pmatrix} 3 & -2 \\ -5 & 4 \end{pmatrix} = \begin{pmatrix} 1\frac{1}{2} & -1 \\ -2\frac{1}{2} & 2 \end{pmatrix}$

c (i) 5 (ii) $\frac{1}{5}\begin{pmatrix} -3 & -10 \\ 2 & 5 \end{pmatrix} = \begin{pmatrix} -\frac{3}{5} & -2 \\ \frac{2}{5} & 1 \end{pmatrix}$

d (i) 0 (ii) no inverse exists

4 $x = 1, \quad y = 3$

5 **a** $x = 1, \quad y = 1$ **b** $x = 2, \quad y = 0$ **c** $x = 1, \quad y = \frac{1}{2}$

d $x = 4, \quad y = 1$ **e** $x = 5, \quad y = 2$ **f** $x = 1, \quad y = \frac{1}{2}$

6 $x = 16, \quad y = 9$

7 $x = 9, \quad y = 5$

8 $x = -3, \quad y = 0$

Coordinates and graphs

Part 1 Points and axes

1 **a** (3, 3) **b** (3, -2)
c (-1, -2) **d** ($-2\frac{1}{2}$, 3)
e Blackshaw **f** Banksands
g Criffell **h** Meurthill
i (3, 0), (4, -1)
j (-3, 2), (-2, 1)
k (0, -2), (1, 2)

2

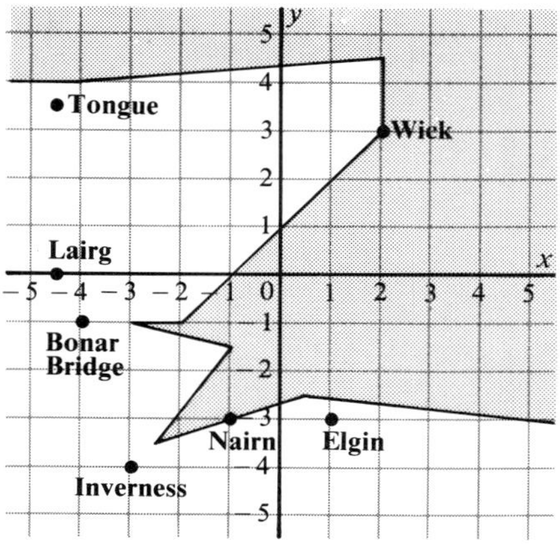

3 (2, -1)
4 (3, -1)
5 (2, 3), (3, 1)
6 (3, 0), (3, 5)
7 (4, 3), (3, 0), (0, 1)
8 (-2, 3), (4, 1), (0, -3)
9 For example, (0, 1), (1, 1), (2, 3)
The straight line $y = 2x - 1$.

10 **a** *A* (20, 10, 50)
B (60, 40, 50)
C (45, 30, 50)
D (10, 50, -25)
E (75, 20, 75)
F (65, 55, 25)
G (60, 35, $62\frac{1}{2}$)
H (15, 20, 15)

b (60, 5, 100)
(40, 40, 25)
(20, 40, 0)
(25, 50, 25)
(55, 30, 80)
(20, 55, -25)
(5, 35, -40)
(65, 15, 85)

Part 2 Directed numbers

1 **a** -2°C
b 2°C
c Perth, by 7 degrees

2 **a** 310 metres **b** 260 metres

3 **a** 55 years
b AD 69

4 **a** (i) £41·30
(ii) £12·00
b (i) £1·40
(ii) £18·20

5 **a** 5
b $^{-}2$
c 7
d $3\frac{1}{2}$
e $\frac{1}{2}$
f $^{-}\frac{1}{2}$
g $^{-}4\frac{1}{2}$
h $^{-}5\frac{1}{4}$
i $5\frac{1}{2}$
j $^{-}6\frac{3}{4}$

6 **a** 2 **b** $^{-}2$ **c** 5
d $^{-}4$ **e** $^{-}5$ **f** 1
g $^{-}2$ **h** 0 **i** $^{-}3$

7 **c** $^{-}12$ **d** 12 **e** $^{-}6$
f 15 **g** $^{-}10$ **h** 3

8 **a** $^{-}21$ **b** 24 **c** $^{-}30$
d 18 **e** 56 **f** $^{-}6$
g 8 **h** $^{-}8$ **i** $^{-}4$
j $^{-}5$ **k** $^{-}3$ **l** $^{-}3$

9 **a** 10 **b** $^{-}4$ **c** 8 **d** $^{-}18$
e $^{-}2$ **f** $^{-}24$ **g** $^{-}2$ **h** $^{-}63$
i 5 **j** 16 **k** $^{-}10$ **l** 35

10 **a** 4 **b** $^{-}4$ **c** 4
d 6 **e** $^{-}4$ **f** 5
g 5 **h** 2 **i** $^{-}6$
j $^{-}6$ **k** $^{-}16$ **l** 50

Coordinates and graphs

Part 3 Relations

1 **a** Rose
b Sadie, Kate
c 3
d Judy, Kate
e niece
f cousin

2 **a**

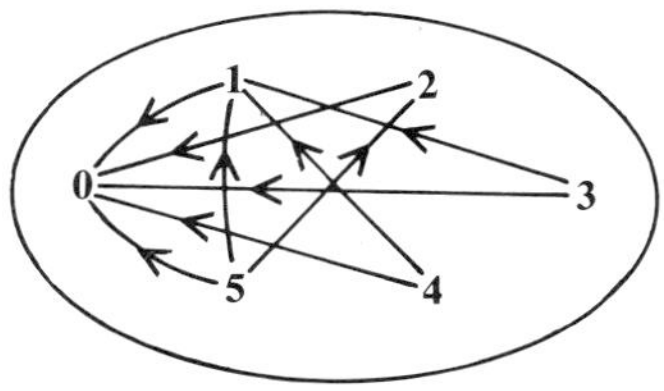

b

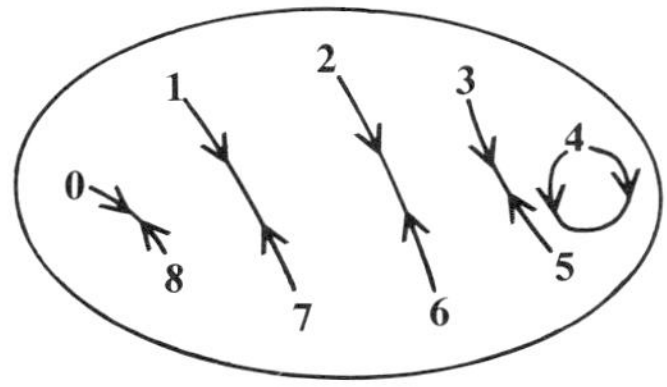

3 **a**

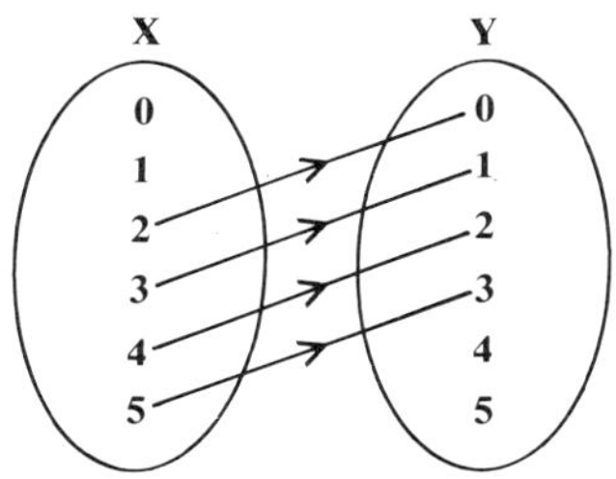

b

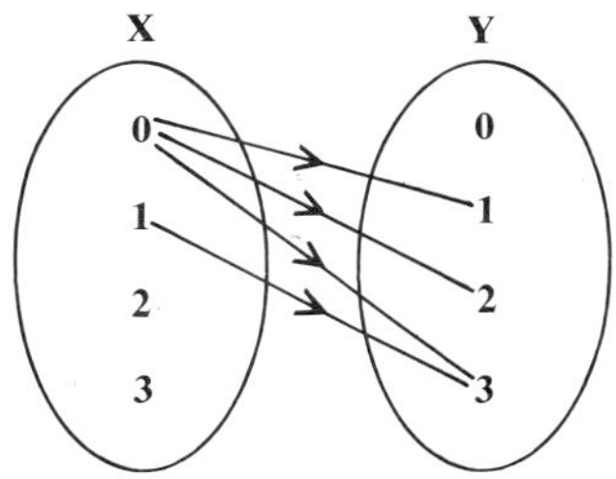

4 **a** $a = 3$ $b = 9$
$c = 17$ $d = 32$

b $e = 9$ $f = 5$
$g = 24$ $h = 14$

5 **a**

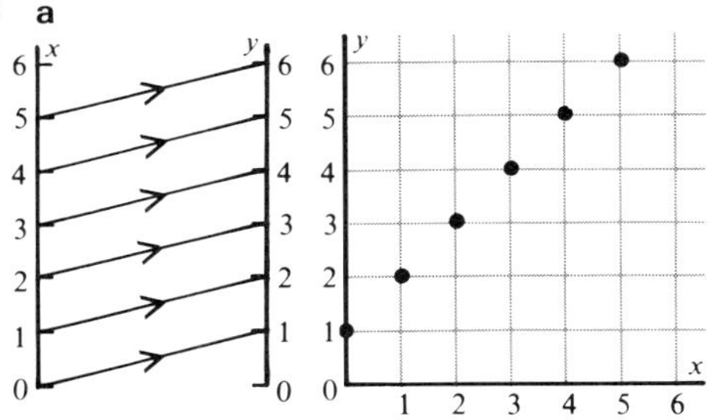

b

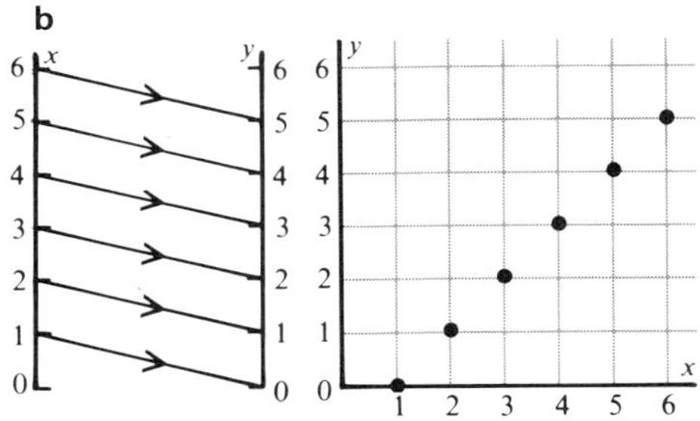

c

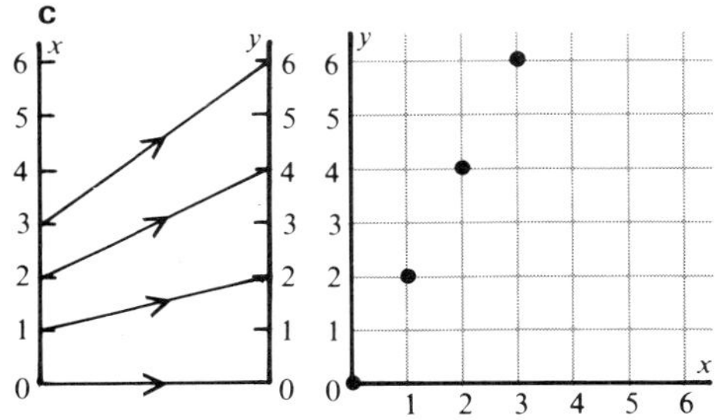

d

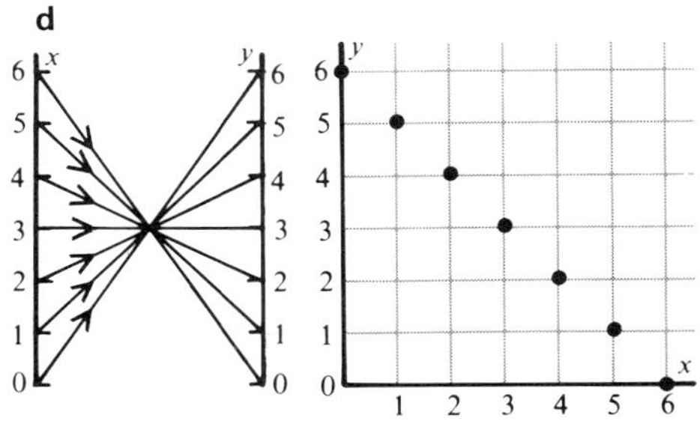

6 **a** $x \to x + 3$ **b** $x \to 5 - x$ **c** $x \to 3x$
d $x \to x + 2$ **e** $x \to 2x$ **f** $x \to 5 - x$

Coordinates and graphs

7 **a** 20 **b** 24
c 15 **d** 0
e 100 **f** 4
g 8 **h** 9 **i** $1\frac{1}{2}$

8 **a** 110 miles
b 152 miles
c 1984 km

9 **a** 3.2 metres
b 70 metres
c 120 km/h

10 **a** (i) none (ii) £2·40
b 30 miles
c 30 pence

Part 4 Straight lines

1 **a** (0, −1), (1, 1), (2, 3), (3, 5), (4, 7), (5, 9)
b $y = 2x - 1$

2 **a**

x	1	2	3	4	5	6
y	$3\frac{1}{2}$	4	$4\frac{1}{2}$	5	$5\frac{1}{2}$	6

b $y = \frac{1}{2}x + 3$

3 **a**

x	−1	0	1	2	3	4
y	−3	−1	1	3	5	7

c (3, 5)

4 **a** on **b** on
c off **d** on

5 **a, e, f**

6

x	0	1	2	3	4	5
y	5	7	9	11	13	15

$3\frac{1}{2}$ hours

7

t	0	10	20	30	40	50
y	20	15	10	5	0	−5

a 30 min
b 40 min
c 20°C

8

t	0	2	4	6	8	10
V	10	14	18	22	26	30

a 20 cm^3
b 7 min
c 10 cm^3

9

M, kg	0	10	20	30	40	50
L, cm	20	22	24	26	28	30

a 27 cm
b 15 kg
c 20 cm

10

	a Gradient	**b** y-intercept	**c** Equation
A	2	2	$y = 2x + 2$
B	3	−2	$y = 3x - 2$
C	$\frac{1}{2}$	−2	$y = \frac{1}{2}x - 2$
D	1	1	$y = x + 1$
E	−2	4	$y = -2x + 4$
F	$-\frac{1}{2}$	5	$y = -\frac{1}{2}x + 5$

11 **a** $y = 2x + 2$ **b** $y = x + 3$
c $y = -\frac{1}{2}x + 4$ **d** $y = -x$

12 **a** gradient = 3; y-intercept = 5
b $y = 3t + 5$
c 35 amps

13 **a** gradient = 4; y-intercept = −5
b $y = 4x - 5$
c 107 DM
d The bank charges a commission of 5 DM.

14 **a** 2
b 2
c 63.4°

15 **a** 71.6° **b** 76.0° **c** 26.6° **d** 45.0°

16 **a** (0, 6) and (4, 0) **b** (0, 2) and (4, 0)
c (0, 5) and (6, 0) **d** (0, −3) and (5, 0)

17 $x = 2, y = 3$

18 **a**

x	−1	0	1	2	3
$y = x + 2$	1	2	3	4	5
$y = 2x - 1$	−3	−1	1	3	5

b $x = 3, y = 5$

19 **a** no solutions **b** infinite solutions

20 **b** (i) Hyravan is cheaper for 6 days (£80 compared with £95).
(ii) Flexicar is cheaper for 2 days (£35 compared with £40).

Coordinates and graphs

Part 5 Parabolas

1 d (i) A translation of $\begin{pmatrix} 0 \\ 4 \end{pmatrix}$. (ii) A translation of $\begin{pmatrix} 4 \\ 0 \end{pmatrix}$.

2 a

x	-1	0	1	2	3	4	5
x^2	1	0	1	4	9	16	25
$-4x$	$+4$	0	-4	-8	-12	-16	-20
$+3$	$+3$	$+3$	$+3$	$+3$	$+3$	$+3$	$+3$
y	8	3	0	-1	0	3	8

b (i) $x = 1$ or 3
(ii) $x = 0$ or 4
(iii) $x = 2$ only

c (1, 0) and (4, 3)

3 a

x	-2	-1	0	1	2	3	4
x^2	4	1	0	1	4	9	16
$-2x$	$+4$	$+2$	0	-2	-4	-6	-8
-3	-3	-3	-3	-3	-3	-3	-3
y	5	0	-3	-4	-3	0	5

b $x = -1$ or 3

c $(0, -3)$ and (3, 0)

4 a

x	-3	-2	-1	0	1	2	3	4
x^2	9	4	1	0	1	4	9	16
$-x$	$+3$	$+2$	$+1$	0	-1	-2	-3	-4
-3	-3	-3	-3	-3	-3	-3	-3	-3
y	9	3	-1	-3	-3	-1	3	9

b $x = -1.30$ or 2.30

c $x = -1$ or 3

5 a

x	-2	-1	0	1	2	3	4
3	3	3	3	3	3	3	3
$+2x$	-4	-2	0	$+2$	$+4$	$+6$	$+8$
$-x^2$	-4	-1	0	-1	-4	-9	-16
y	-5	0	3	4	3	0	-5

b $-0.62 < x < 1.62$

6 a

x	0	1	2	3	4	5	6
48	48	48	48	48	48	48	48
$-2x$	0	-2	-4	-6	-8	-10	-12
$-x^2$	0	-1	-4	-9	-16	-25	-36
y	48	45	40	33	24	13	0

b 48 metres

c 60 metres

Coordinates and graphs

7 **a** For the shot:

x	0	1	2	3	4	5
8	8	8	8	8	8	8
$+4x$	0	+4	+8	+12	+16	+20
$-x^2$	0	−1	−4	−9	−16	−25
y	8	11	12	11	8	3

For the slope:

x	0	1	2	3	4	5	6	7	8
y	8	7	6	5	4	3	2	1	0

b 40 metres
c 50 metres

Part 6 Other curves

1 **a**

x	−9	−6	−3	−2	−1	0	1	2	3	6	9
y	−2	−3	−6	−9	−18	∞	18	9	6	3	2

b

x	−5	−2	1	2	3	4	5	6	7	10	13
y	−2	−3	−6	−9	−18	∞	18	9	6	3	2

c

x	−9	−6	−3	−2	−1	0	1	2	3	6	9
y	−6	−7	−10	−13	−22	∞	14	5	2	−1	−2

d (i) a translation of $\begin{pmatrix} 4 \\ 0 \end{pmatrix}$ (ii) a translation of $\begin{pmatrix} 0 \\ 4 \end{pmatrix}$

2 **a**

x	1	2	3	4	5	6
y	12	6	4	3	2.4	2

b £8000
c £3

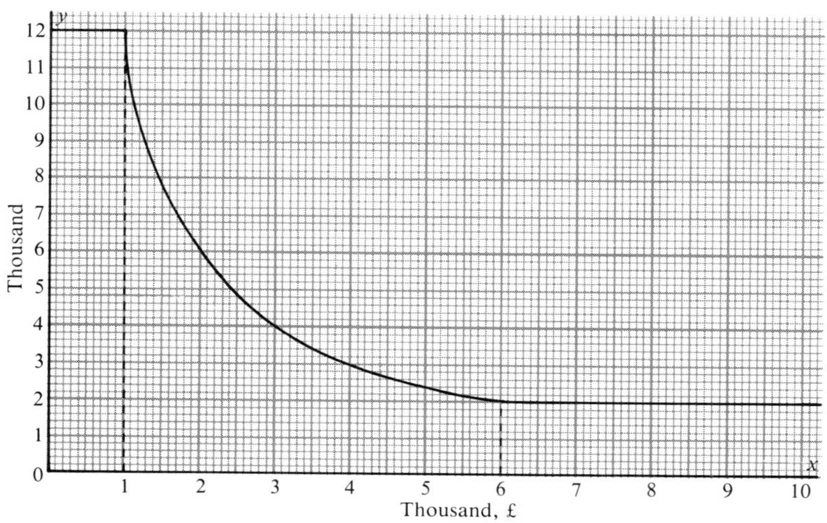

Coordinates and graphs

3 a

x	0	1	2	3	4	5	6
$x + 2$	2	3	4	5	6	7	8
y	12	8	6	4.8	4	3.4	3

b 3 units **c** 12 units **d** 4.8 units

4 a

x	-3	-2	-1	0	1	2	3
x^3	-27	-8	-1	0	1	8	27
$-4x$	$+12$	$+8$	$+4$	0	-4	-8	-12
y	-15	0	3	0	-3	0	15

b

x	-3	-2	-1	0	1	2	3
x^3	-27	-8	-1	0	1	8	27
$-5x$	$+15$	$+10$	$+5$	0	-5	-10	-15
$+2$	$+2$	$+2$	$+2$	$+2$	$+2$	$+2$	$+2$
y	-10	4	6	2	-2	0	14

c

x	-1	0	1	2	3	4
x^3	-1	0	1	8	27	64
$-3x^2$	-3	0	-3	-12	-27	-48
$+4$	$+4$	$+4$	$+4$	$+4$	$+4$	$+4$
y	0	4	2	0	4	20

5 a

t	0	1	2	3	4	5
t^3	0	1	8	27	64	125
$-8t$	0	-8	-32	-72	-128	-200
$+15t$	0	$+15$	$+30$	$+45$	$+60$	$+75$
$+10$	$+10$	$+10$	$+10$	$+10$	$+10$	$+10$
θ	10	18	16	10	6	10

b (i) 18.2°C (ii) 5.9°C

c After 3 minutes and 5 minutes.

d

t	0	1	2	3	4	5
ϕ	8	10	12	14	16	18

e After 2.5 minutes.

f After 1 minute.

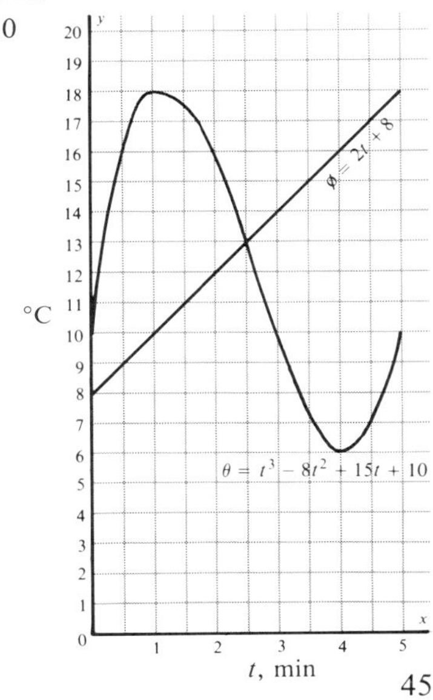

Coordinates and graphs

Part 7 Areas under lines and curves

1 **a** 40 squares
b £48

2 **a** 100 m^2

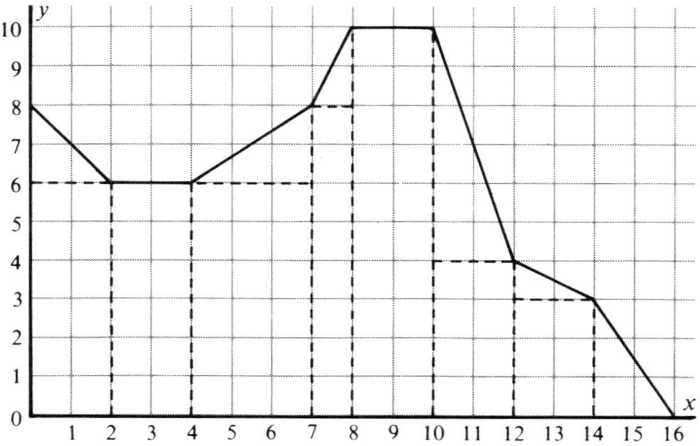

b £425
c 48.8 metres; £117 approx.

3 Approx 30 squares.

4 **a** 630 squares; 52.5 units
b 630 squares; 52.5 units
c 930 squares; 77.5 units
d 780 squares; 65 units

5 **a** 60 square units
b 15°C

6 **a** 20 litres **b** 24 kg **c** £200
d 33 km **e** 520 m **f** 100 kg

7 **a** 3600 m = 3.6 km
b 20 m/s

8 **a** 2550 litres
b 85 litres/min

9 **a** 830 m approx
b 14 m/s approx

10 **a**

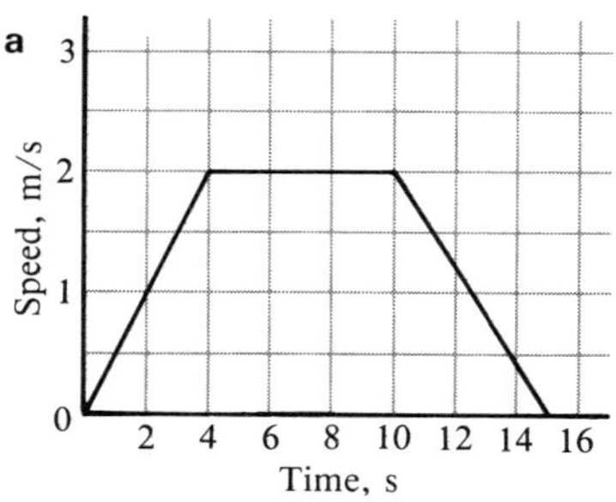

b 21 m; 1.4 m/s

11

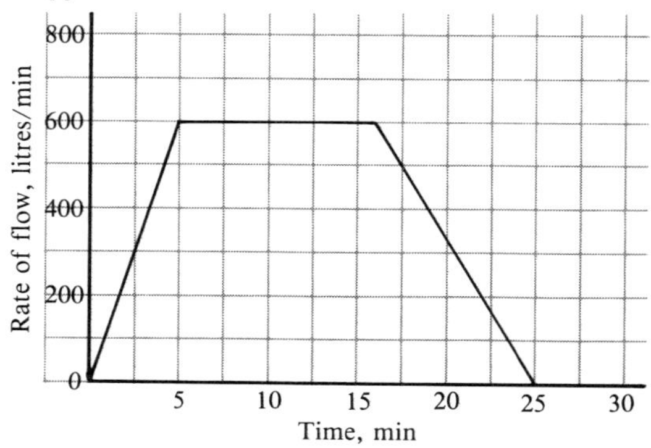

a 11 100 litres
b 444 litres/min

Part 8 Rates of change

Constant rates of change

1 **a** 8°C/min **b** 3 m^3/h **c** 10 kg/s

2 280 litres

3 720 metres

4 26°C

5 40 litres

Coordinates and graphs

Average rates of change

6 **a** $3\frac{1}{3}$°C/min **b** $13\frac{1}{3}$°C/min
c $7\frac{1}{2}$°C/min **d** $-8\frac{1}{3}$°C/min

7 **a** 7.5 m/s **b** 3.5 m/s
c 8.0 m/s **d** 5.7 m/s

Instantaneous rates of change

8 **a** $7\frac{1}{2}$°C/min **b** 0°C/min **c** -2°C/min

9 **a** $-7\frac{1}{2}$ amps/s **b** 6 amps/s **c** 0 amps/s
These are approximate values.

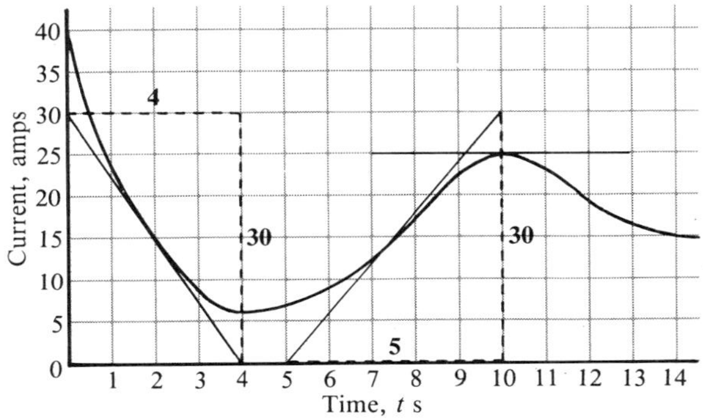

10 **a** -3 m/s **b** 0 m/s
c 1 m/s

Part 9 Distance, speed and acceleration

Distance-time graphs

1 **a** 30 cm
b 5 sec
c 6 cm/s
d 10 s
e 10 s
f 3 cm/s

2 **a** 600 m; 5 min
b 120 m/min
c 5 minutes
d (i) 800 m (ii) 200 m
e 40 m/min
f 20 min; 40 m/min

3 **a** 8 h; 75 km/h
b 2 h; 100 km/h
c 1 h; 400 km
d 4 h; 100 km/h
e 4 h; 300 km

4

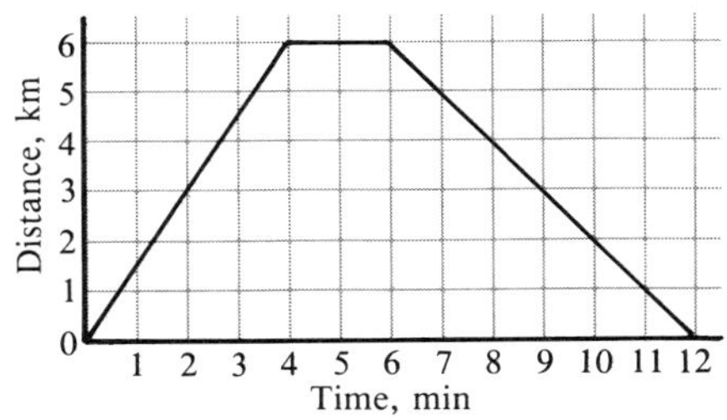

a $1\frac{1}{2}$ km/min **b** 1 km/min

5

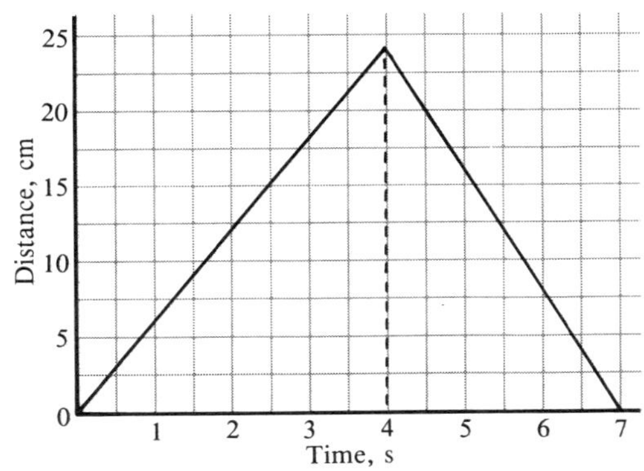

8 cm/s on return

Coordinates and graphs

6 **a** 2 m/s
b 3 m

7 **a** $2\frac{1}{2}$ cm/s **b** 0 cm/s **c** 8 cm/s
d 12 s
e 0 cm/s
f 30 cm

8 **a** $11\frac{1}{2}$ m/s **b** $7\frac{1}{2}$ m/s
c 0 m/s
d $7\frac{1}{2}$ m/s

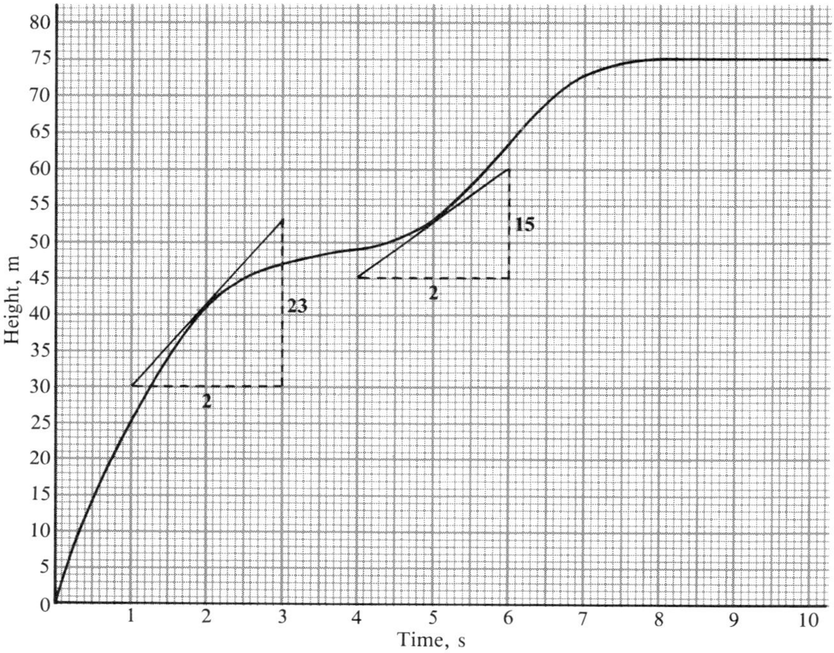

9 **a**

t	0	1	2	3	4	5	6
$12t$	0	12	24	36	48	60	72
$-2t^2$	0	-2	-8	-18	-32	-50	-72
h	0	10	16	18	16	10	0

b (i) 8 m/s (ii) 0 m/s (iii) 4 m/s downwards
c 18 metres; 3 seconds
d 12 m/s

Speed-time graphs

10 **a** 5 m/s
b $1\frac{1}{4}$ m/s^2
c 10 metres
d 0 m/s^2
e 20 metres

11 **a** 21 metres
b 36 metres
c 3.6 m/s
d (i) $\frac{1}{2}$ m/s
(ii) 0 m/s^2
(iii) $-2\frac{1}{2}$ m/s^2

12

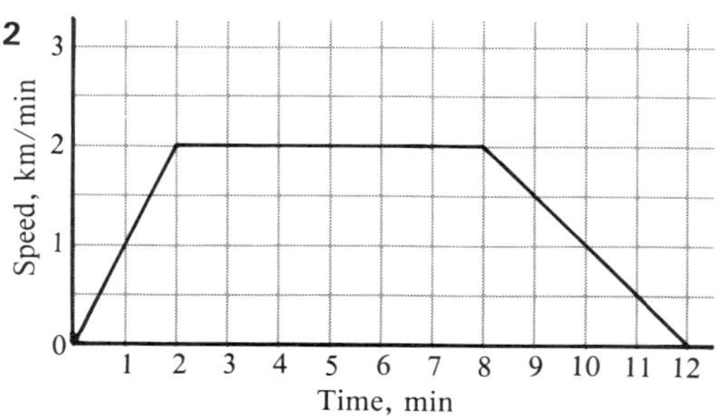

a 18 km
b $1\frac{1}{2}$ km/min
c 1 km/min^2
d $\frac{1}{2}$ km/min^2

Coordinates and graphs

13

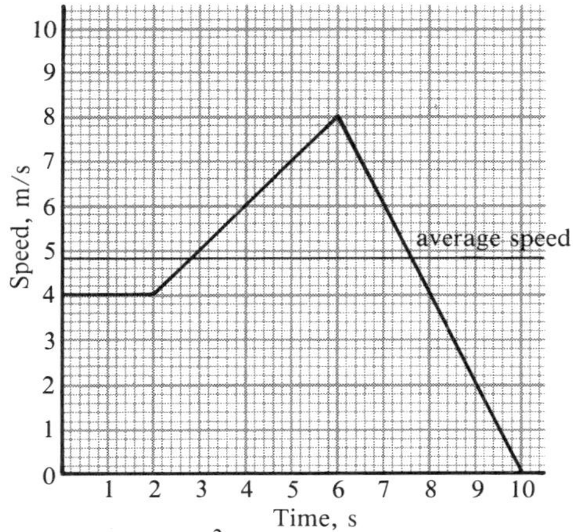

a (i) 0 m/s^2 (ii) 1 m/s^2
(iii) -2 m/s^2
b 48 m
c 4.8 m/s^2

14 **a** (i) 10 m/s^2
(ii) 0 m/s^2
(iii) $-7\frac{1}{2}$ m/s^2
b about 347 metres
c approx 24.8 m/s

15

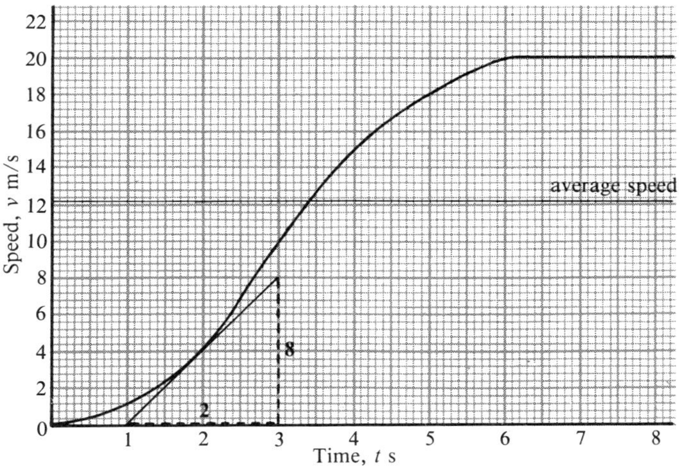

a 4 m/s^2
b $t > 6$ s
c The steepest tangent to the curve occurs when $t = 3$.
d 98 m
e 12.3 m/s

16

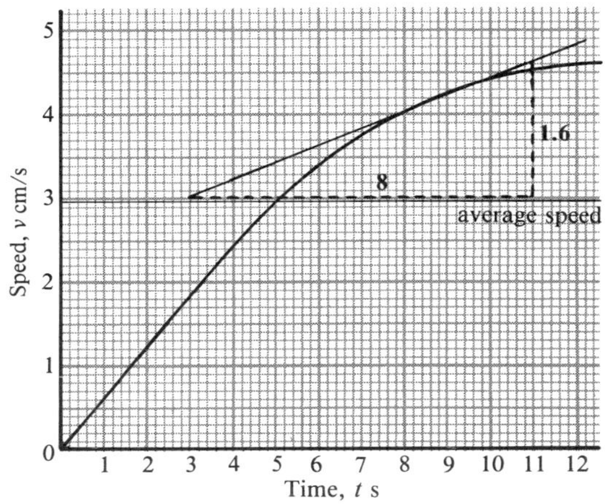

a 0.2 cm/s^2
b As t approaches 12 seconds.
c 35.4 cm
d 2.95 cm/s

Coordinates and graphs

17

t	0	1	2	3	4	5	6	7
7	7	7	7	7	7	7	7	7
$+6t$	0	+6	+12	+18	+24	+30	+36	+42
$-t^2$	0	−1	−4	−9	−16	−25	−36	−49
v	7	12	15	16	15	12	7	0

a 7 m/s
b 7 s
c $t = 3$ s
d -2 m/s^2
e 81.7 m
f 11.7 m/s

18

t	0	1	2	3	4	5	6	7	8
64	64	64	64	64	64	64	64	64	64
$-t^2$	0	−1	−4	−9	−16	−25	−36	−49	−64
v	64	63	60	55	48	39	28	15	0

a 64 m/s
b 8 s
c (i) 0 m/s^2
(ii) -8 m/s^2
d 341 m
e 34.1 m^3

Algebra

Part 1 Simplification and substitution

1 **a** $6x + 5y$ **b** $9m + 5n$
c $3x + 1$ **d** $14y + 4z$
e $7a - 12b + 5$ **f** $7y + z - 12$

2 **a** 9 **b** 14 **c** 1
d 1 **e** 8 **f** 21

3 **a** $11x + y$, 68 **b** $5z - 2y$, 11
c $3x - 2$, 16 **d** $5x + y - 5z$, 17
e $6x - 2y - 10z$, 2
f $2z - 2y + 1$, 3

4 **a** 150 g **b** 650 g **c** 290 g

5 **a** £6 **b** £12 **c** £18·50

6 **a** 6 min **b** 13 min **c** 10 min

7 **a** 125 pence **b** 69 pence **c** 117 pence

8 **a** 202 **b** 504
c $121\frac{1}{2}$

9 **a** $15p^2q$ **b** $30x^2y$
c $24\,mn$ **d** $21abc$
e $24pq^2$ **f** $12s^2t^2$
g $5ab + ac$ **h** $3mq$
i $4xy + xz$ **j** $2tv$
k $3ac + bc$ **l** $3xy + 3yz$

10 **a** 44 **b** 10 **c** 20
d 18 **e** 36 **f** 16

11 **a** £480 **b** £400 **c** £880

Algebra

12 a 2　b $1\frac{1}{2}$　c 2.4

13 a 38 min　b 44 min　c 74 min

14 a 1000　b 480
c 5200

15 a $2x + 3y$
b 16 cm
c 8 cm

16 Perimeter $= 5x$
20 cm

17 a Area of one row $= 3h + 4t$
b Area of 5 rows $= 15h + 20t$
c 55 m^2

Part 2 Expansions and factors

1 a $x^2 + 6x$　b $x^2 + 3x$

2 a $x^2 - 5x$　b $3x + 6$　c $8x - 12$
d $6x^2 + 3x$　e $x^3 + 3x^2 - 2x$　f $2x^3 - 8x^2 + 2x$
g $2x^3 - x^2 + 3x$　h $15xy - 20x$　i $3x^2 + 6xy + 9xz$

3 a $2(x + 3)$　b $2(x - 5)$　c $2(4x + 1)$
d $x(x - 3)$　e $y(y + 5)$　f $2y(y - 4)$
g $3z(2z + 3)$　h $2x(y - 3z)$　i $xy(x + 2)$

4 $x^2 + 7x + 10$

5 a $x^2 + 10 + 21$　b $x^2 + 2x - 24$　c $x^2 - 9x + 20$
d $x^2 - 6x + 9$　e $2x^2 + 11x + 12$　f $6x^2 + 17x + 5$
g $8x^2 - 6xy - 9y^2$　h $6x^2 + xy - 12y^2$　i $4x^2 - 4xy + y^2$

6 a $(x + 5)(x + 1)$　b $(x + 4)(x + 1)$　c $(x + 5)(x - 2)$
d $(x - 5)(x + 2)$　e $(x + 5)(x - 3)$　f $(x - 9)(x + 2)$
g $(x - 4)(x - 2)$　h $(x - 6)(x - 5)$　i $(x - 24)(x - 6)$

7 a $x^2 - 25$　b $x^2 - 9$　c $9x^2 - 16$

8 a $(x - 6)(x + 6)$　b $(x - 4)(x + 4)$　c $(2x - 7)(2x + 7)$
d $(3x - 5)(3x + 5)$　e $(x - 1)(x + 1)$　f $(x - \frac{1}{2})(x + \frac{1}{2})$

9 a 9400　b 746 000　c 208
d 57　e 2　f 9

10 a $x(x - 3)$　b $2(3x + 2)$　c $(x + 4)(x + 2)$
d $(x - 3)(x + 3)$　e $x(x - 9)$　f $(x - 7)(x - 2)$
g $2x(x - 4)$　h $(x - 2)(x + 2)$　i $x(x - 4)$
j $(x - 6)(x + 2)$　k $x(x - 1)$　l $(x - 9)(x + 8)$

Part 3 Equations

1 a 6　b 10　c 4　d 16
e 9　f 15　g 4　h 36
i 4　j 3　k 8　l 12

2 a 4　b 4
c 3　d $1\frac{1}{2}$
e $1\frac{1}{3}$　f 1
g 2　h $1\frac{1}{2}$
i 4　j $\frac{1}{2}$
k 8　l 10

3 40°

4 36°

5 £6

6 a 6
b 18 cars; 9 vans

7 a $9m + 4n$
b 85
c $m = 4$

8 a $3m + M$
b $60m + 20M$
c $15m + 5M = 900$ gives $M = 60$ grams

Algebra

9 **a** $h + 5r$
b $h + 24r$
c $h = 12$ cm

10 **a** $x + 1$ and $x - 7$
b $x = 64$

11 **a** 2 **b** 6 **c** 15 **d** 16
e $4\frac{1}{2}$ **f** $5\frac{1}{2}$ **g** 4 **h** $6\frac{2}{3}$
i $13\frac{1}{2}$ **j** $3\frac{3}{10}$ **k** 12 **l** $\frac{4}{15}$

12 40 miles

13 72 miles

14 288 metres

Simultaneous equations

15 $x = 1, y = 3$

16 **a**

x	0	1	2	3
$y = x + 1$	1	2	3	4
$y = 3x - 1$	-1	2	5	8

$x = 1, y = 2$

b

x	0	1	2	3	4
$y = \frac{1}{2}x + 2$	2	$2\frac{1}{2}$	3	$3\frac{1}{2}$	4
$y = 2x - 1$	-1	1	3	5	7

$x = 2, y = 3$

c

x	0	1	2	3	4	5
$y = x + 3$	3	4	5	6	7	8
$y = 6 - x$	6	5	4	3	2	1

$x = 1\frac{1}{2}, y = 4\frac{1}{2}$

17 **a** $x = 2, y = 1$ **b** $x = 3, y = 2$ **c** $x = -2, y = 3$
d $x = 2, y = -1$ **e** $x = 1, y = 1$ **f** $x = 2, y = 1$

18 **a** $x = 4, y = 10$ **b** $x = 1, y = 2$ **c** $x = 1, y = 2$
d $x = -3, y = 1$ **e** $x = 5\frac{1}{2}, y = 16$ **f** $x = 1\frac{1}{4}, y = 5\frac{3}{4}$

19 37 and 24

20 $a = 40$ pence, $c = 15$ pence

21 $p = 5$ pence, $m = 7$ pence

Quadratic equations

22 **a** $x = 1, x = 3$

b

x	0	1	2	3	4	5
x^2	0	1	4	9	16	25
$-5x$	0	-5	-10	-15	-20	-25
$+4$	$+4$	$+4$	$+4$	$+4$	$+4$	$+4$
y	4	0	-2	-2	0	4

$x = 1$ and $x = 4$

Algebra

c

x	0	1	2	3	4	5	6
x^2	0	1	4	9	16	25	36
$-7x$	0	-7	-14	-21	-28	-35	-42
$+9$	$+9$	$+9$	$+9$	$+9$	$+9$	$+9$	$+9$
y	9	3	-1	-3	-3	-1	3

$x = 1.70$ and $x = 5.30$

23 **a** 2, 7 **b** -4, 5 **c** -6, -5
d -1, 1 **e** 0, 7 **f** 0, -3

24 **a** -1, -5 **b** -1, -7 **c** 2, 1
d 4, 2 **e** 5, 2 **f** 9, 2
g -7, 1 **h** 5, -3 **i** 8, -1
j -7, 3 **k** 5, 4 **l** -10, 2

25 **a** -4, 4 **b** 0, 5 **c** 0, 7
d 0, 4 **e** -2, 2 **f** -1, 1
g 0, 1 **h** 0, -1 **i** 0, -2
j -3, 3 **k** 0, 9 **l** 0, -9

26 4, -6

27 $x = 3$ cm

28 $x = 8$ m

29 $x = 2$ m or 4 m

30 $x = 3$ m

31 **a** $-\frac{1}{2}$, -1 **b** $-\frac{1}{5}$, -1 **c** $\frac{1}{6}$, 1
d $\frac{1}{2}$, $\frac{1}{3}$ **e** $-\frac{3}{5}$, -1 **f** $\frac{1}{3}$, 5
g $-\frac{1}{2}$, 1 **h** $-1\frac{1}{3}$, 1 **i** $2\frac{1}{4}$, $-\frac{1}{2}$

32 **a**

x	0	1	2	3	4	5
x^2	0	1	4	9	16	25
$-4x$	0	-4	-8	-12	-16	-20
$+2$	$+2$	$+2$	$+2$	$+2$	$+2$	$+2$
y	2	-1	-2	-1	2	7

x	0	1	2	3	4	5
y	-2	-1	0	1	2	3

b $x = 1$ or 4

Part 4 Inequalities

1 **a** $x \geqslant 1$
b $-2 \leqslant x \leqslant 3$
c $x < 2$
d $-3 < x < 1$

2 **a** $x \geqslant 6$ **b** $x \leqslant 6$
c $x < 3\frac{1}{4}$ **d** $x > 4$
e $x \leqslant 6\frac{1}{2}$ **f** $x < 1$
g $x \leqslant -2$ **h** $x > -2$
i $x > \frac{1}{2}$ **j** $x \geqslant 6$
k $x < 6$ **l** $x \leqslant -2\frac{1}{2}$

3 4

4 4

5 $1 \leqslant x \leqslant 4$

6 **a** $0 \leqslant x \leqslant 4$ **b** $1 \leqslant x \leqslant 3$
c $x \leqslant 0$ and $x \geqslant 4$ **d** $x \leqslant 1$ and $x \geqslant 3$

Algebra

7 a

x	0	1	2	3	4	5	6
x^2	0	1	4	9	16	25	36
$-6x$	0	-6	-12	-18	-24	-30	-36
$+5$	$+5$	$+5$	$+5$	$+5$	$+5$	$+5$	$+5$
y	5	0	-3	-4	-3	0	5

x	0	1	2	3	4	5	6
y	-3	-2	-1	0	1	2	3

c (i) $1.44 < x < 5.56$ (ii) $x = 1.44$ or 5.56
(iii) $x < 1.44$ or $x > 5.56$

Part 5 Regions and linear programming

1 a $x \leqslant 2$ **b** $y \geqslant 2$ **c** $x > 3$
d $1 \leqslant y \leqslant 3$ **e** $x \geqslant 1$ and $y \geqslant 4$ **f** $x \geqslant -1$ and $y \leqslant 2$

2 a

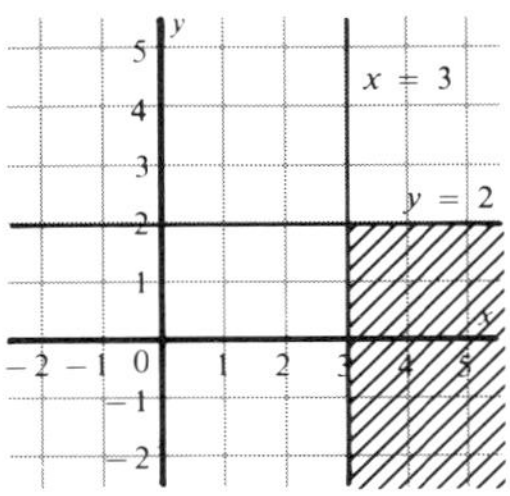

b

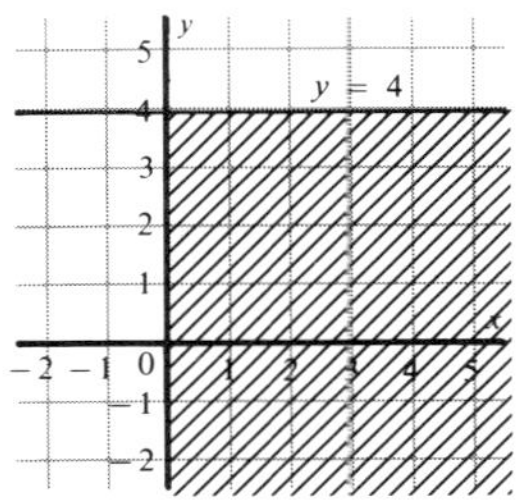

c

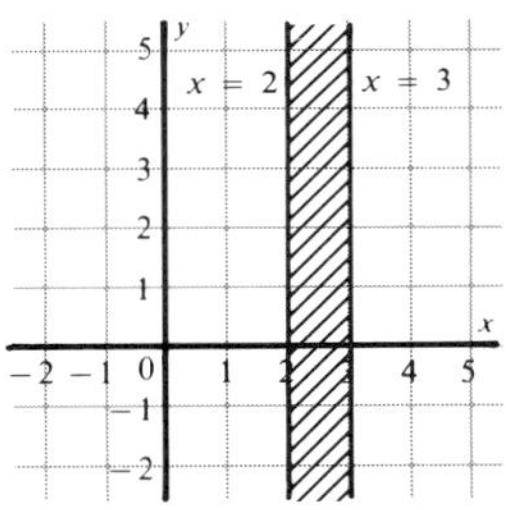

d

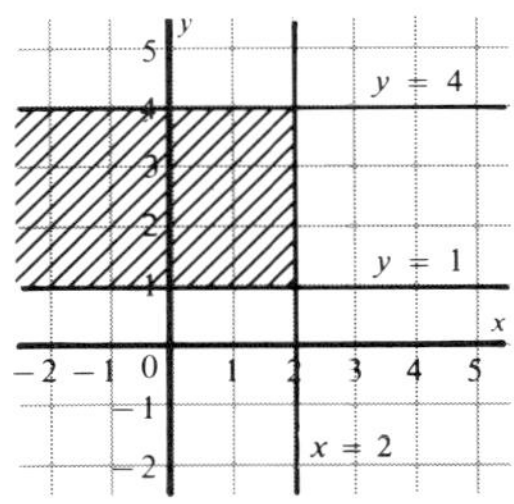

e

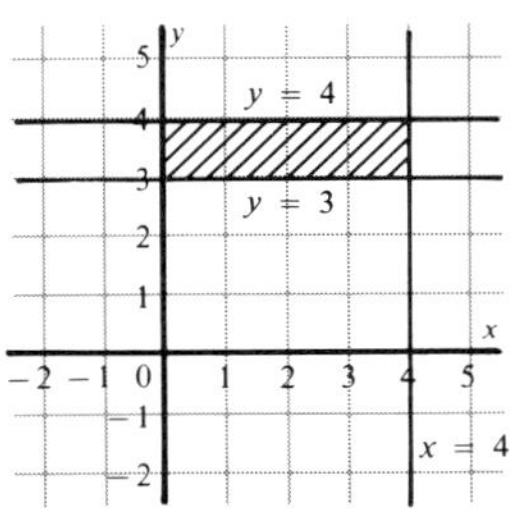

f

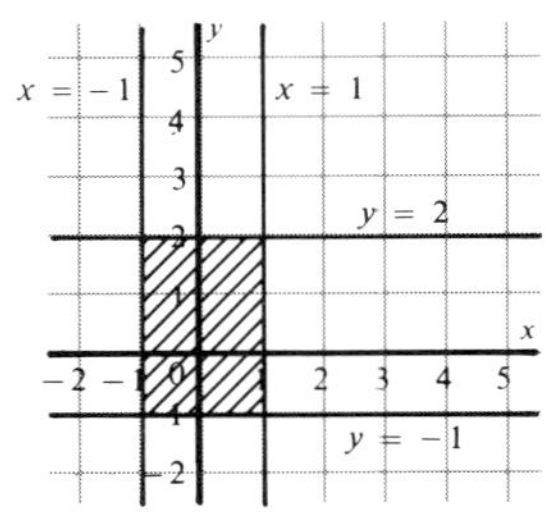

3 a $x + y \geqslant 4$ and $y \leqslant 2$
b $x + y \leqslant 3$ and $y \leqslant x + 2$
c $y \leqslant x + 2$, $y \leqslant 2x$ and $y \geqslant 2 - \frac{1}{2}x$

Algebra

4 a

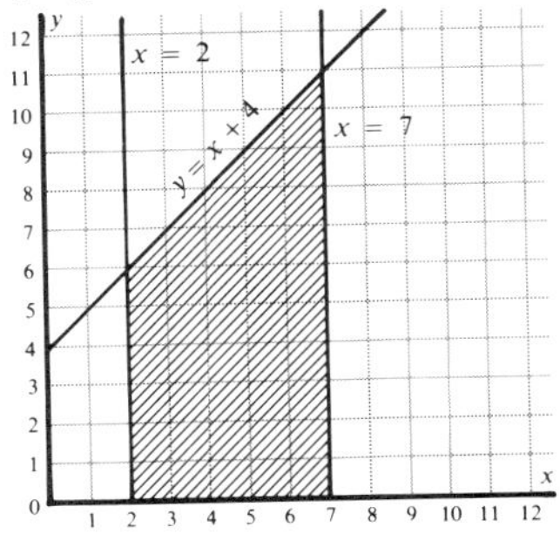

b

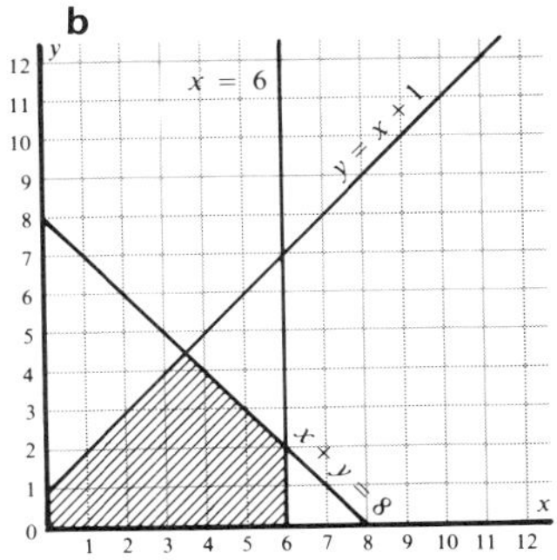

c

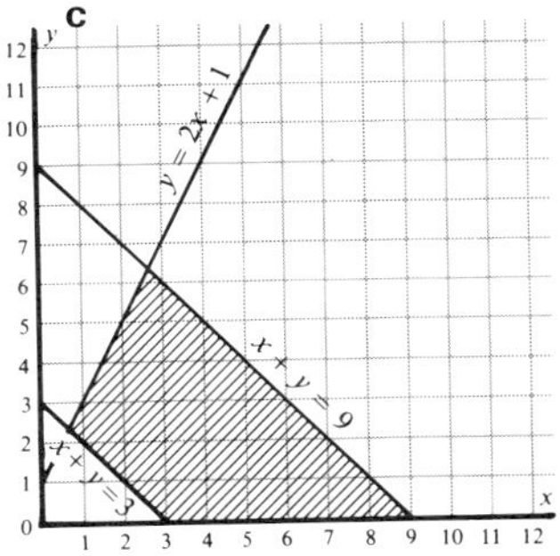

d

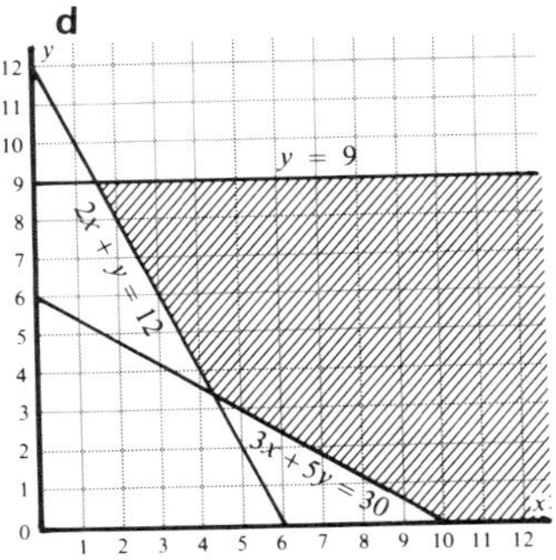

e

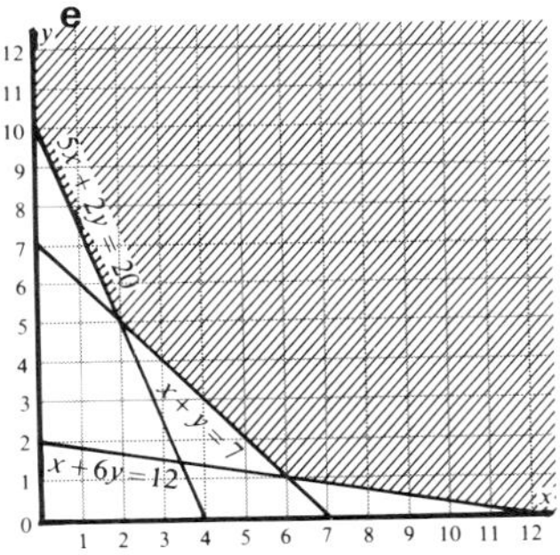

f

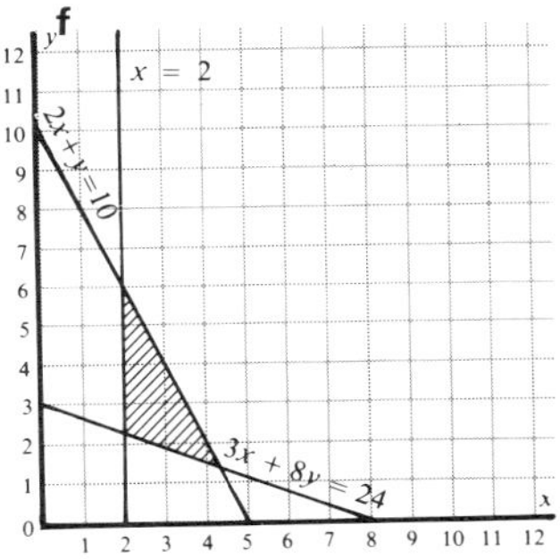

5

Corner	(2, 4)	(5, 4)	(5, 1)
Value of $3x - y$	2	11	14

a (5, 1)

b (2, 4)

6

Corner	(1, 2)	(2, 4)	(4, 3)	(3, 1)
Value of $5x + 2y$	9	18	26	17

a (4, 3)

b (1, 2)

7 a

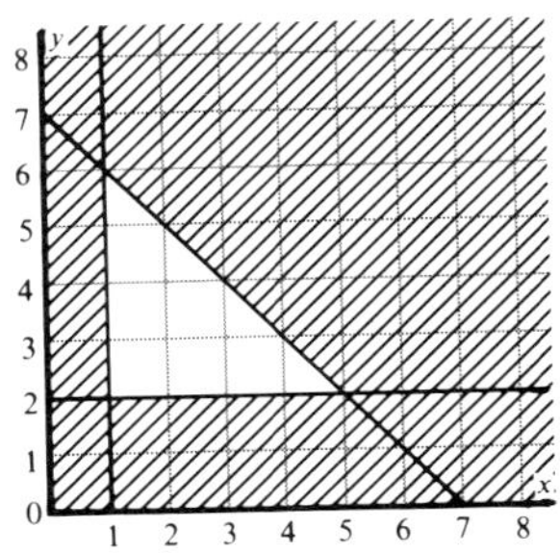

Corner	(1, 2)	(1, 6)	(5, 2)
Value of $2x + y$	4	8	12

Minimum value at (1, 2)

Algebra

b

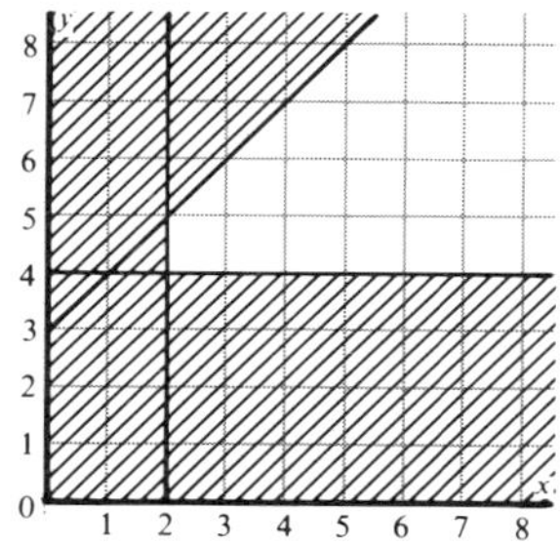

Corner	(2, 4)	(2, 5)
Value of $3x + 4y$	22	26

Minimum value at (2, 4).

c

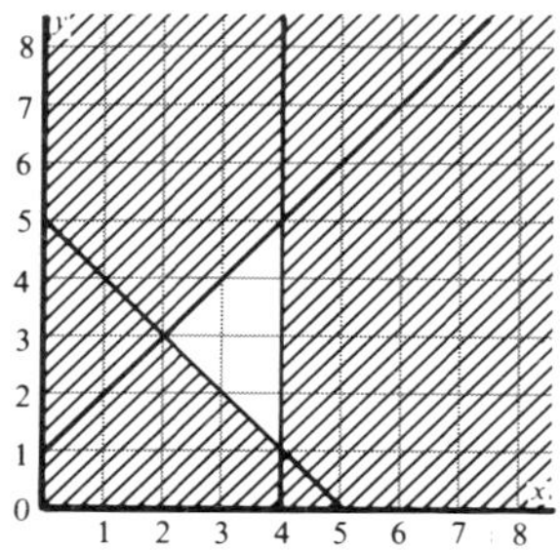

Corner	(2, 3)	(4, 1)	(4, 5)
Value of $5y - x$	13	1	21

Maximum value at (4, 5).

d

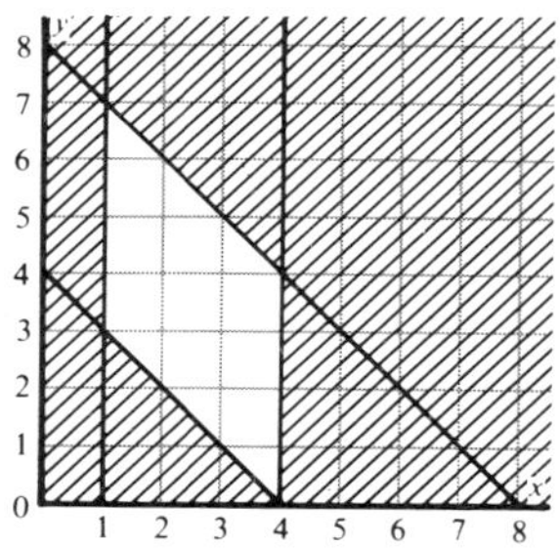

Corner	(1, 3)	(1, 7)	(4, 0)	(4, 4)
Value of $4x - y$	1	-3	16	12

Maximum value at (4, 0).

8

a Possibilities	(2, 2)	(3, 2)	(4, 2)	(2, 3)	(3, 3)	(1, 4)
b Total cost, £	28 000	34 000	40 000	36 000	42 000	38 000

c The least cost of £28 000 occurs when two of each type of car are bought.

9 (i) $x \geqslant 2$
(ii) $y \geqslant 3$
(iii) $x + y \leqslant 8$

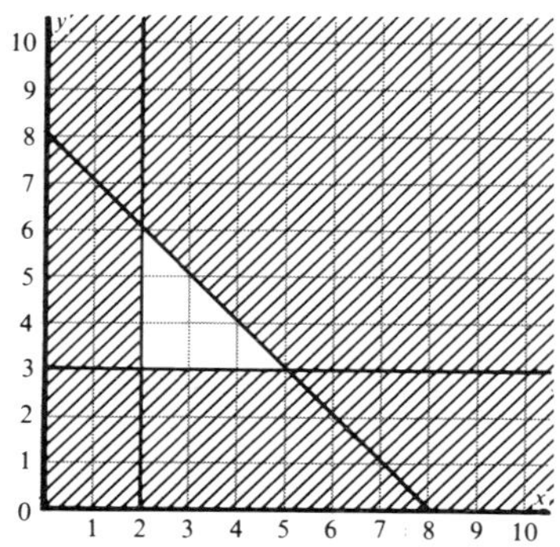

Corner	(2, 3)	(2, 6)	(5, 3)
Cost, £	480	720	840

Minimum cost occurs when 2 double and 3 single windows are fitted.

Algebra

10 **a** $y \geqslant 2$
$y \leqslant x$
$x + y \leqslant 8$

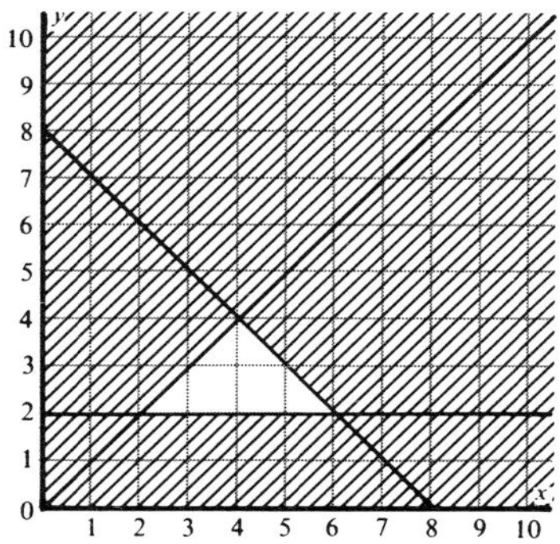

b

Corner	(2, 2)	(4, 4)	(6, 2)
Cost, £	7	14	13

Minimum cost of £7 occurs when 2 metres of each type of wire is bought.

11 **a** $8x + 4y \geqslant 32$
b $x + y \geqslant 6$
c $y \geqslant 2$

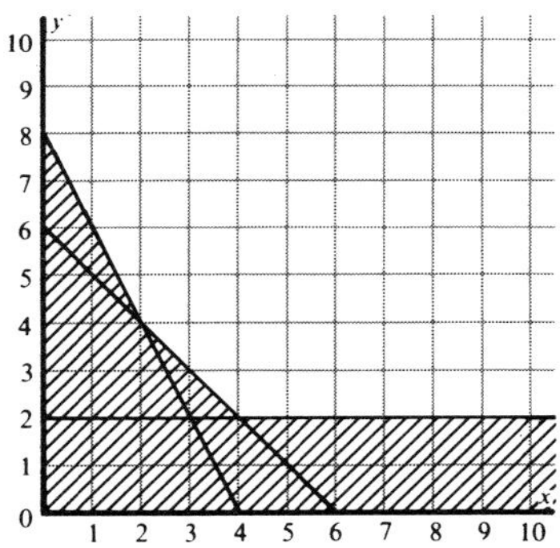

Corner	(0, 8)	(2, 4)	(4, 2)
Cost, £	80	90	120

The minimum cost of £80 occurs when 8 Nauts and no Juggers are used.

12 **a** $x \geqslant 10$
$y \geqslant 5$
$x + y \geqslant 20$
$y \leqslant 2x$

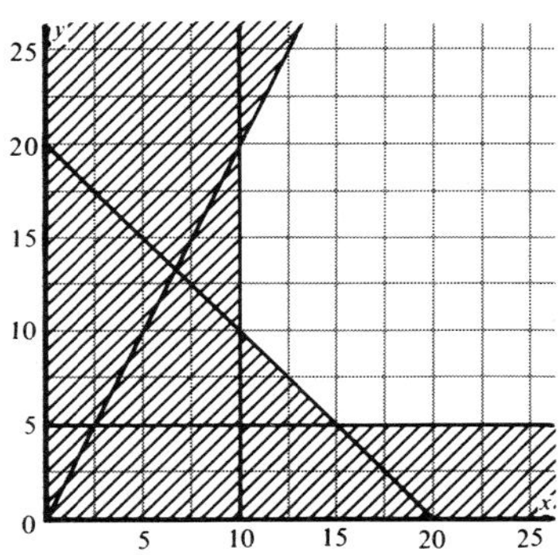

b

Corner	(10, 20)	(10, 10)	(15, 5)
Cost, £	20	15	17

Minimum cost of £15 occurs when 10 m^2 are planted with potatoes and 10 m^2 with beans.

Algebra

Part 6 Flow diagrams and computer programs

1

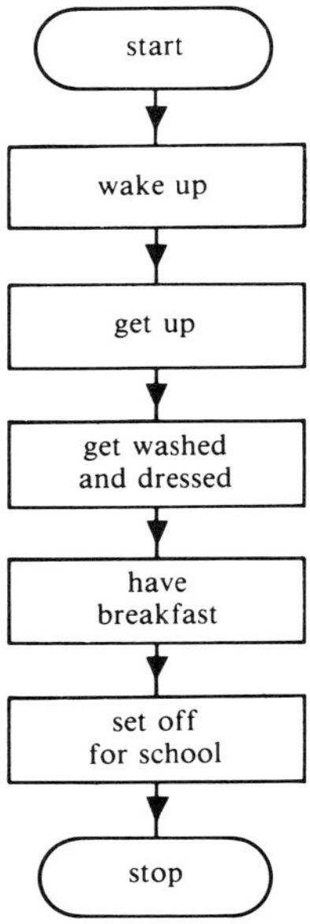

2

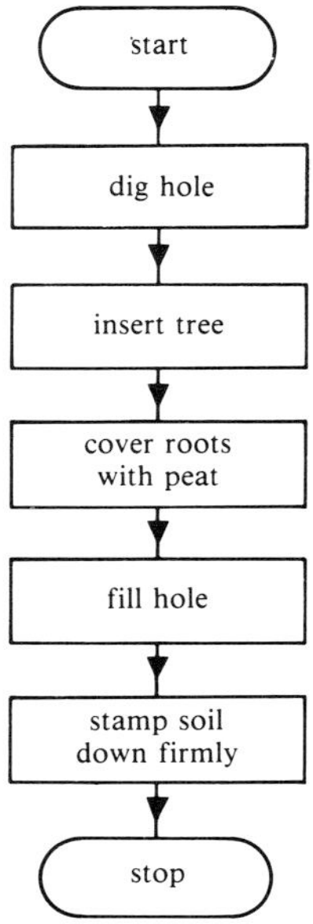

3

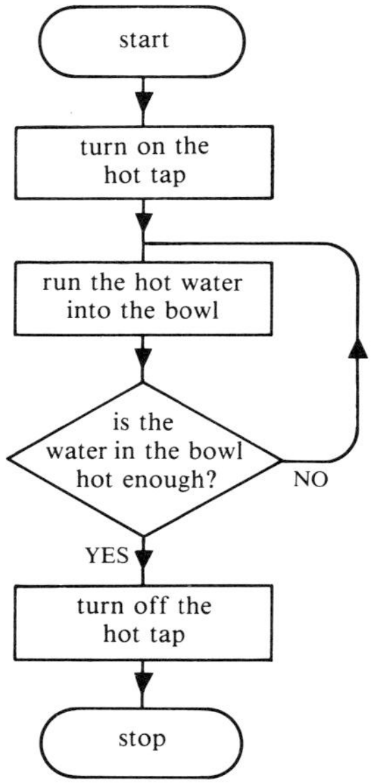

4

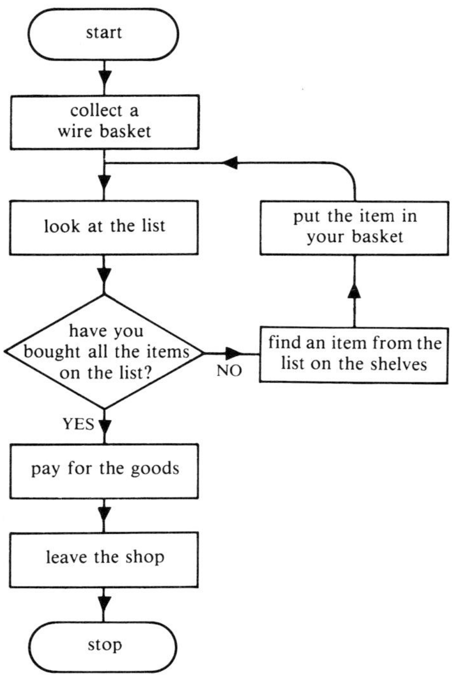

5

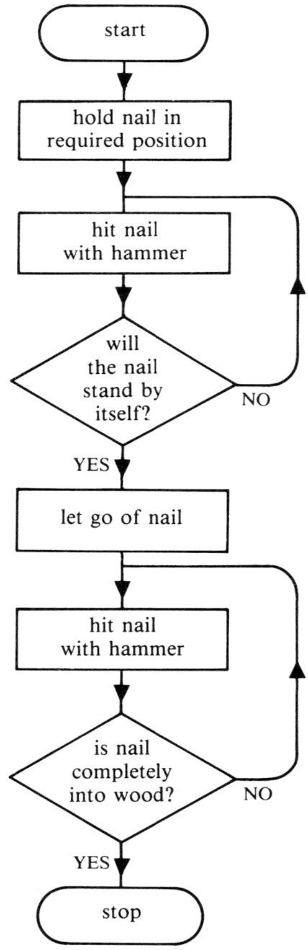

Algebra

6

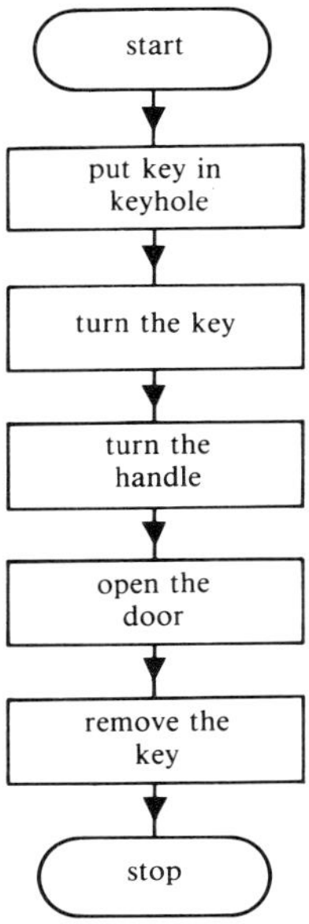

(For some doors, the key may be removed at an earlier stage.)

7

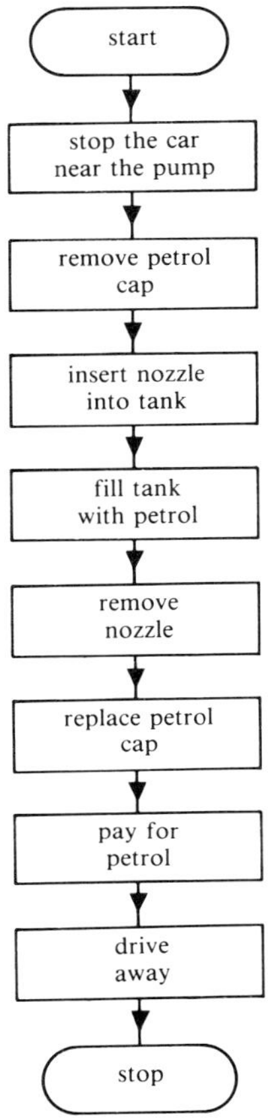

8

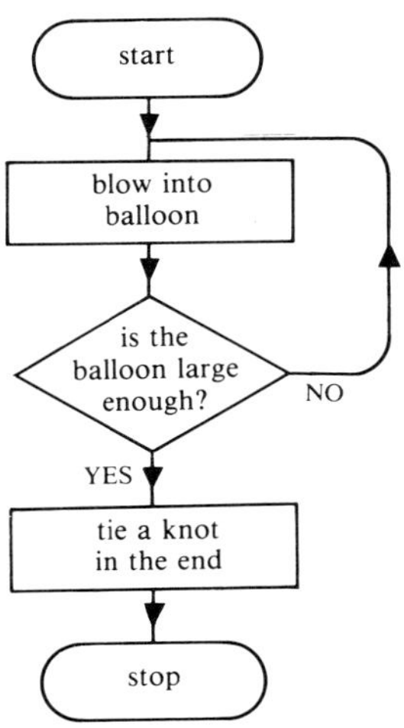

9

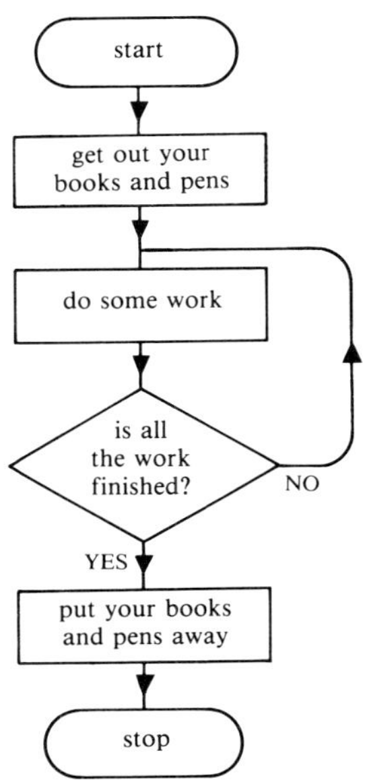

10

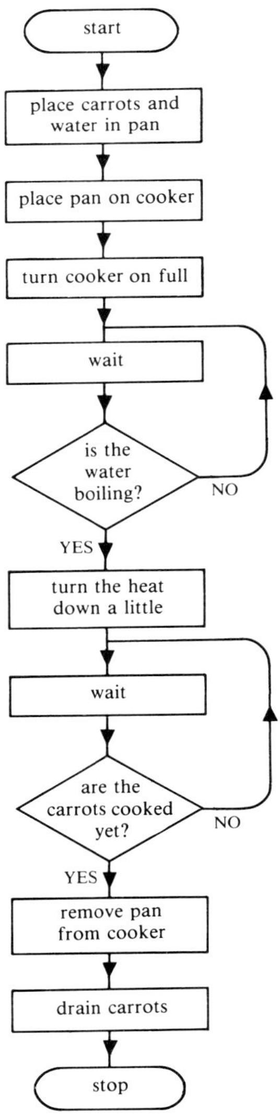

Algebra

11 There are many possibilities. Here is one example for each situation.

a

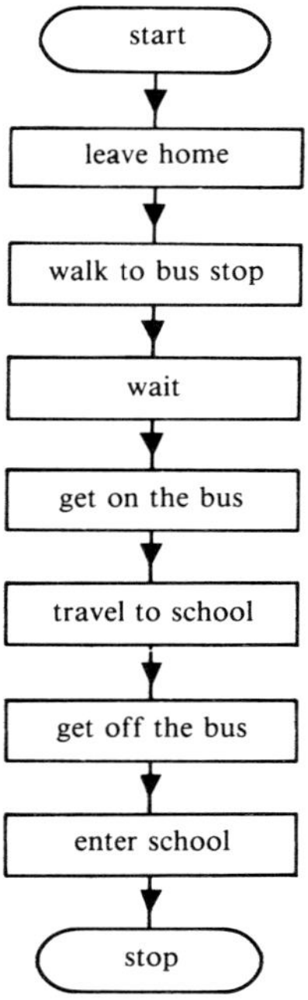

b

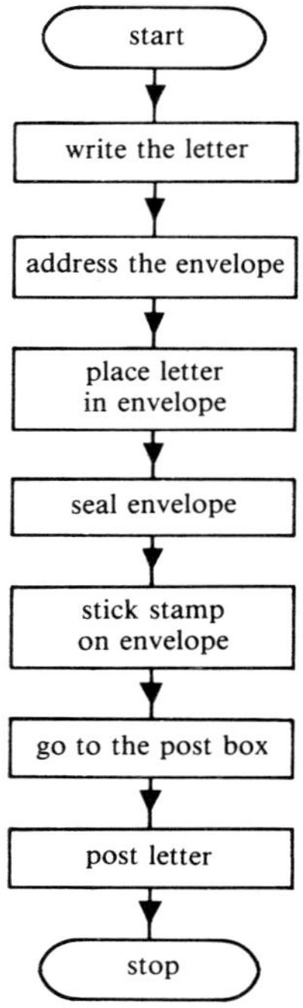

c

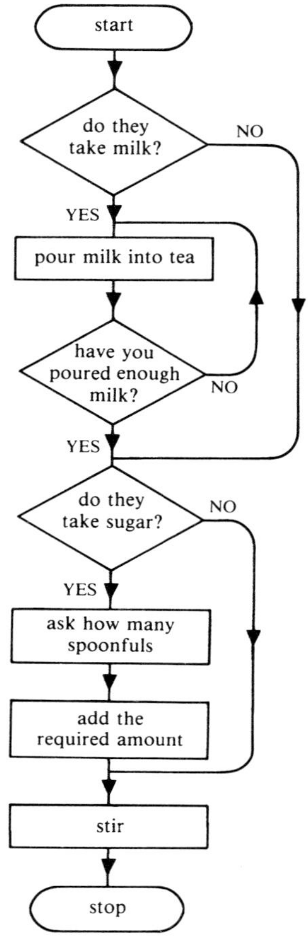

d

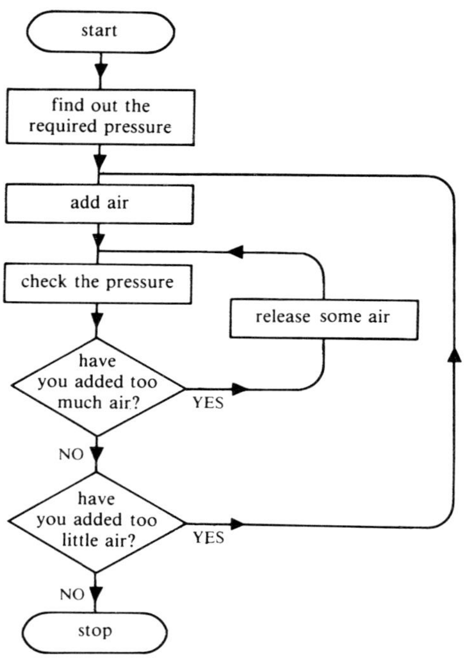

12 **a** $\frac{65}{5} = 13$

b the mean age

c The final value of T is the total of all five ages.

13 **a** £174

b W is his basic weekly wage. X is his overtime pay for the week.

c £4 per hour

d £6 per hour

Algebra

14 **a** $T = 76$

b $T = 99$

c £2 per post; C is the cost of all the posts required.

d £3 per metre; D is the cost of the netting required.

e T is the total cost of the fence.

15 **a** $S = 180, 276, 366, 546$ $T = 10, 18, 24, 28$

b (i) The final value of S is the total cost of all the tins in pence.

(ii) The final value of T is the total number of tins bought.

16 **a**

```
10 INPUT R
20 S=R*R
30 A=3.14*S
40 PRINT A
50 END
```

b A = 78.5 cm^2

17 **a**

```
10 INPUT H
20 T=0.5*H
30 INPUT P
40 T=T+P
50 PRINT T
60 END
```

b T = 4

18 **a**

```
10 T=0
20 FOR N=1 TO 5
30 INPUT M
40 T=T+M
50 NEXT N
60 A=T/5
70 PRINT A
80 END
```

b $A = 60$

19 **a**

```
10 T=0
20 FOR N=1 TO 4
30 INPUT C
40 T=T+C
50 NEXT N
60 X=80-T
70 PRINT X
80 END
```

b $C = 12$

c The total amount of money they have between them.

d Alter line 60 to become $X = 120 - T$.

20 **a**

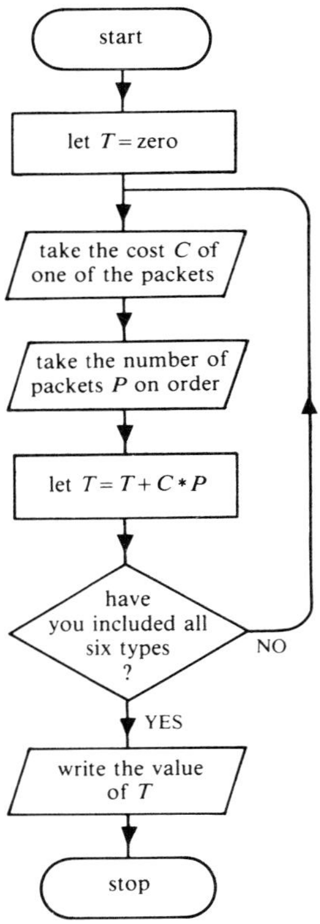

b

```
10 T=0
20 FOR N=1 TO 6
30 INPUT C
40 INPUT P
50 T=T+C*P
60 NEXT N
70 PRINT T
80 END
```

Total cost = £46·80

Algebra

Dry runs

1 $P = 55$ pence

2 $C = £48$

3 $V = 8\ \text{cm}^3$

4 $D = 36$ metres

5 $A = 7.5\ \text{m/s}^2$

6 $C = £23$

7 $I = £16$; $Q = £216$

8 $W = £188$

9 $S = £12$; $B = £54$; $C = £66$

10 $X = 3$; $Y = 2$

11 $A = 53$
This assumes he has been 'out' in each innings.

12 $D = 1$

13 **a** $D = £1{\cdot}60$ **b** $D = 0$

14 **a** not on the line **b** on the line

Sets

1

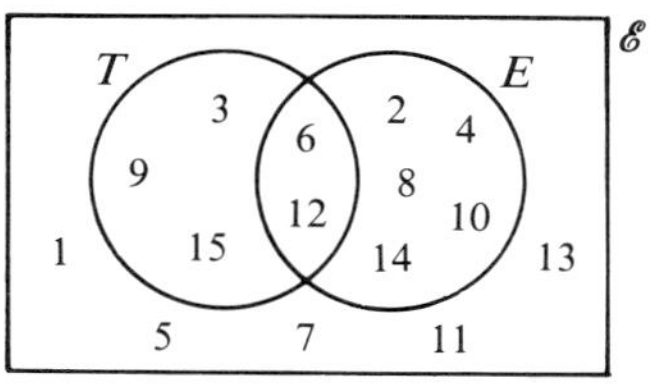

2

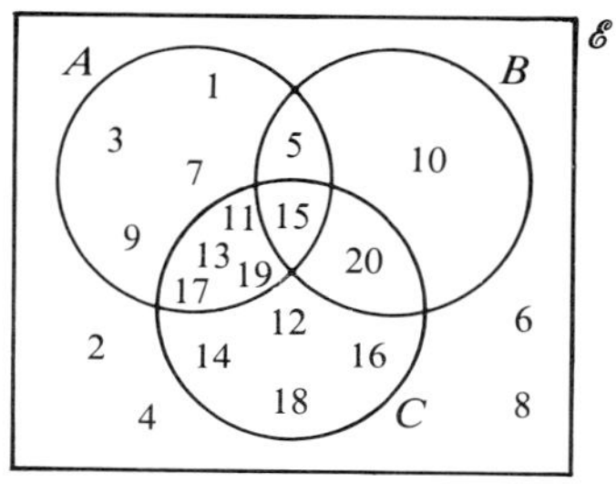

3

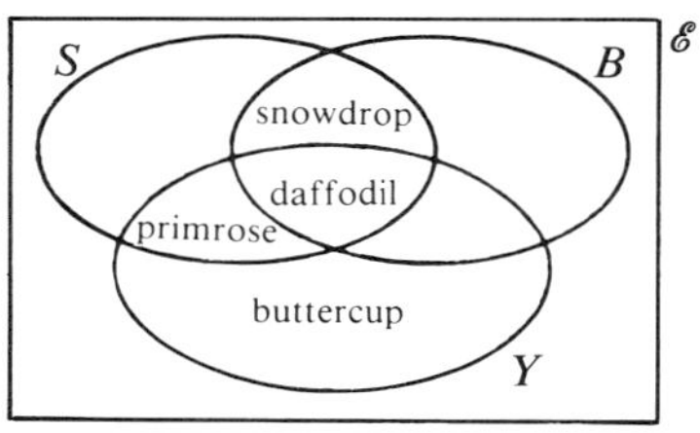

4 **a** true **b** true
c true **d** false
e true **f** false
g false **h** true
i false **j** false
k false **l** false

5 **a** Simon $\in R$ **b** Pam $\in S$
c Jim $\notin T$ **d** Susan $\notin R$
e $R \cap S = \{\text{Jim, Greg}\}$ **f** $S \cap T = \{\text{Susan, Tina}\}$
g $n(R \cup S) = 8$ **h** $n(S \cup T) = 6$
i $n(R') = 7$ **j** $n(S') = 5$
k $n(R \cup S)' = 3$ **l** $T \subset S$

6 **a** $X = \{\text{all babies}\}$
$Y = \{\text{all children}\}$
$Z = \{\text{all young people}\}$

b $P = \{\text{two-door saloon cars}\}$
$Q = \{\text{all saloon cars}\}$
$R = \{\text{estate cars}\}$

c $R = \{\text{all cats}\}$
$S = \{\text{all leopards}\}$
$T = \{\text{African animals}\}$

Sets

7 **a**

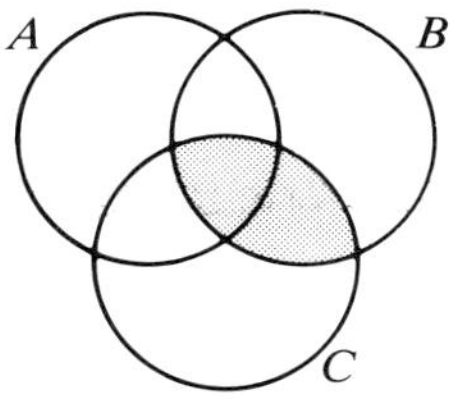

b

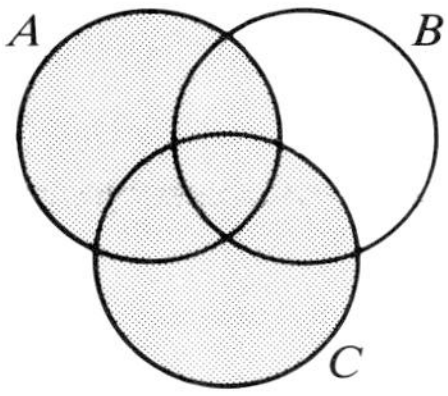

c

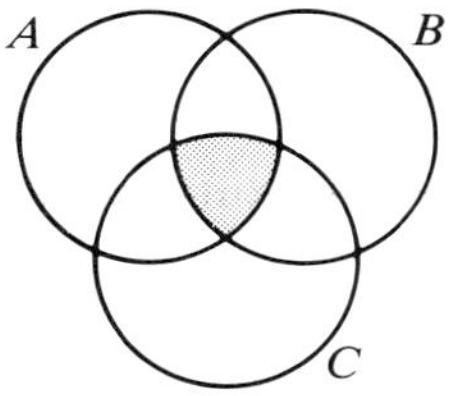

d

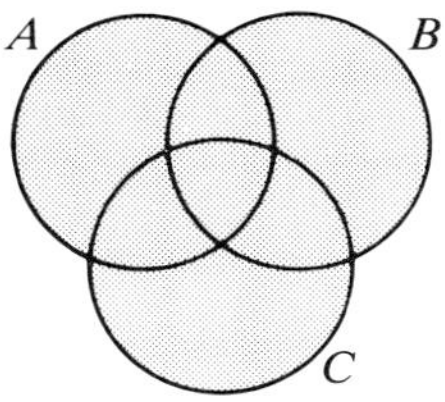

e

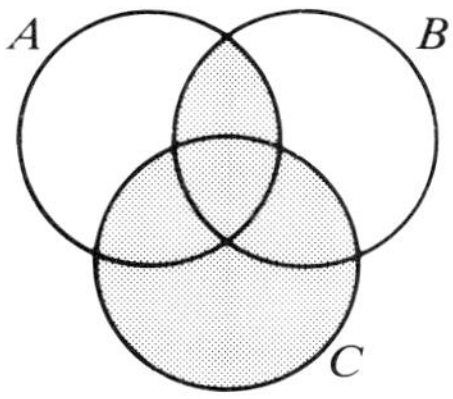

f

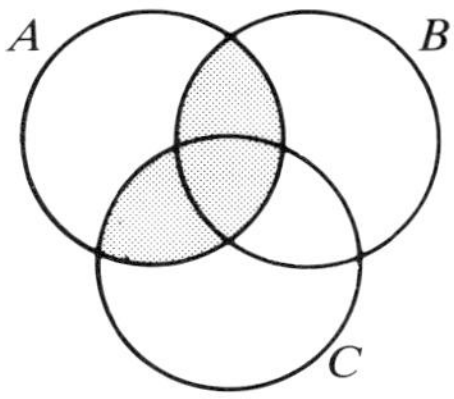

g

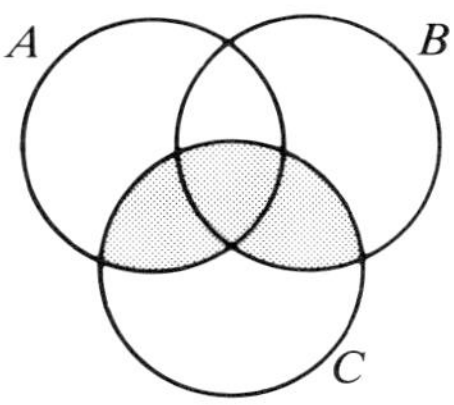

h

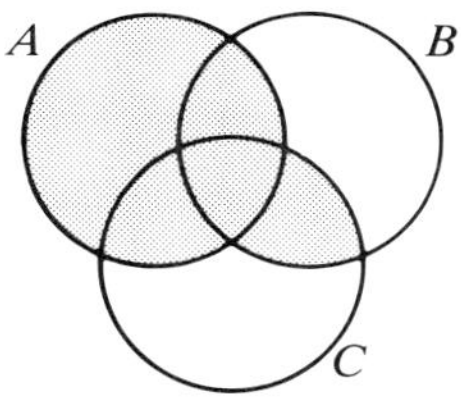

8

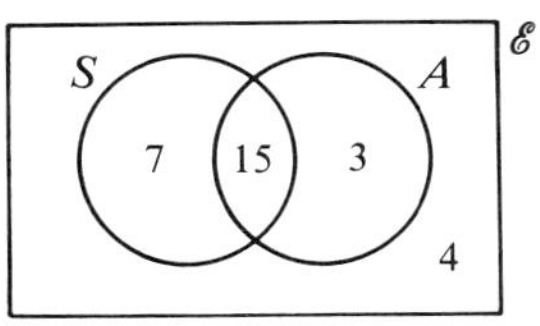

15 pupils study both subjects

9 64 + 17 = 81 applicants for the technician's post

10 12

11 3

12 310

Probability

Part 1 Experimental and theoretical

1 **a** $\frac{14}{20} = 0.7$
b 42

2 **a** 0.85
b 24

3 **a** 0.6
b 9

4 **a** 0.76
b 608

5 **a, b, c, f**

6 **a** $\frac{1}{2}$
b $\frac{1}{4}$
c $\frac{1}{4}$
d $\frac{1}{4}$
e $\frac{8}{52} = \frac{2}{13}$
f $\frac{5}{26}$

7 **a** $\frac{12}{52} = \frac{3}{13}$
b 15

8 **a** $\frac{3}{4}$
b 45

9 **a** 5
b 10

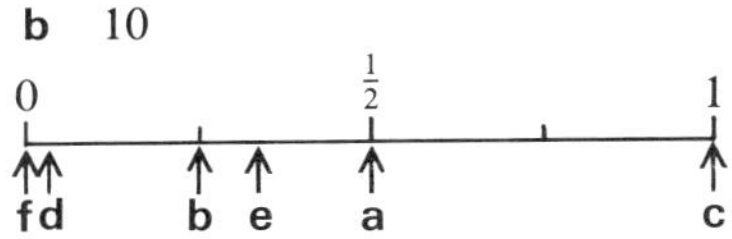

11 **a** 20
b $\frac{1}{2}$

12 **a** 80
b 0.7

Probability

Part 2 Successive events

1 **a** 7
b (i) $\frac{4}{36} = \frac{1}{9}$ (ii) $\frac{5}{36}$ (iii) $\frac{6}{36} = \frac{1}{6}$
c 20

2 **a** (i) $\frac{1}{4}$
(ii) $\frac{1}{2}$
b 30

3 **a** $\frac{2}{8} = \frac{1}{4}$
b 10

4 **b** (i) $\frac{3}{8}$ (ii) $\frac{2}{8} = \frac{1}{4}$
c (i) 15 (ii) 10

5 **a**

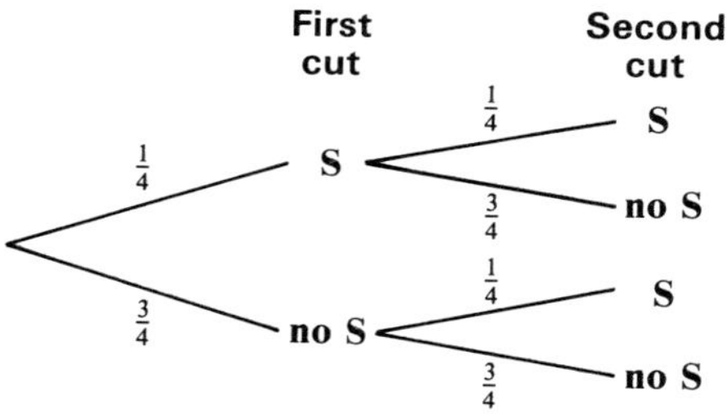

Outcomes	Probabilities
S, S	$\frac{1}{4} \times \frac{1}{4} = \frac{1}{16}$
S, no S	$\frac{1}{4} \times \frac{3}{4} = \frac{3}{16}$
no S, S	$\frac{3}{4} \times \frac{1}{4} = \frac{3}{16}$
no S, no S	$\frac{3}{4} \times \frac{3}{4} = \frac{9}{16}$

b (i) 2 (ii) 12

6

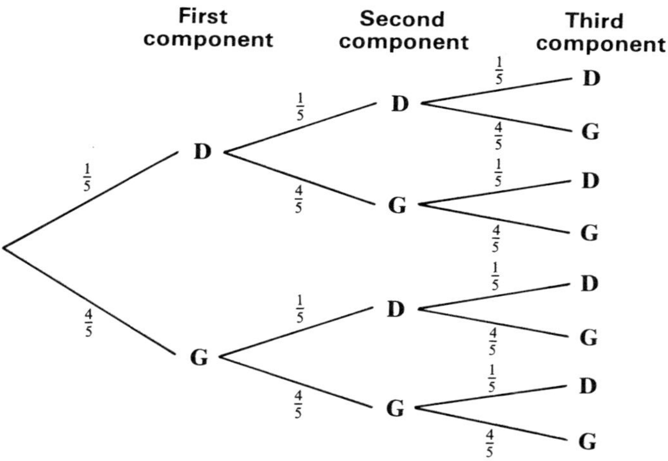

a (i) $\frac{1}{125}$ (ii) $\frac{48}{125}$ (iii) $\frac{64}{125}$
b (i) 4 (ii) 192 (iii) 256

7

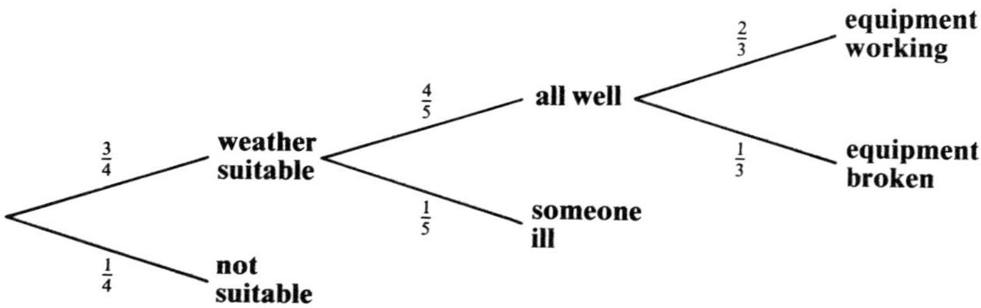

8 days

Probability

8

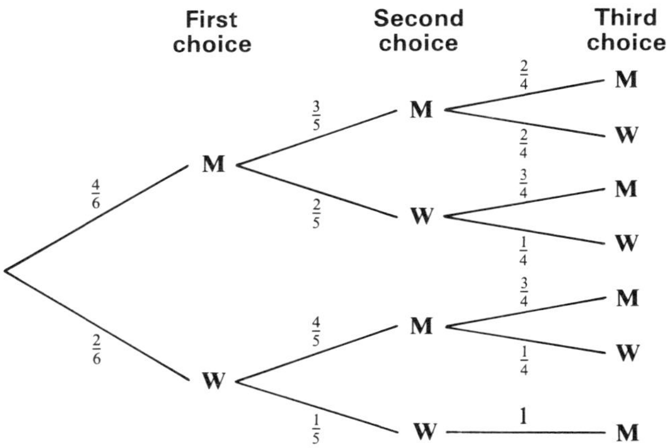

a $\frac{4}{6} \times \frac{3}{5} \times \frac{2}{4} = \frac{1}{5}$

b $(\frac{4}{6} \times \frac{3}{5} \times \frac{2}{4}) + (\frac{4}{6} \times \frac{2}{5} \times \frac{3}{4}) \times (\frac{2}{6} \times \frac{4}{5} \times \frac{3}{4}) = \frac{1}{5} + \frac{1}{5} + \frac{1}{5} = \frac{3}{5}$

Statistics

Part 1 Sampling

1 **a** He is selecting from those who may already prefer that type of margarine.
b Certain types of voters may not have telephones.
c These children will be in the same part of their age group and, at this age, a few months difference in age can produce differences in children's development.

2 **a** Random
b Not random; the sample will mostly include cars registered in the same year, 1982.
c Not random; changes in production might occur at other times on the shift.

3 **a** 125
b 8750
c Increase the number of squares pegged out.

4 **a** 3
b 150
c Increase the number of samples taken.

5 **a** 17.5
b 630
c Sample more classes.

6 $n = 125$

7 500 fish

Part 2 Tabulation

1 counted (discrete) **a, d**
measured (continuous) **b, c, e, f**

2

Number of goals	0	1	2	3	4	Total
Frequency	8	8	7	5	2	30

3

Time late, minutes	0 – 2	2 – 4	4 – 6	6 – 8	8 – 10	Total
Frequency	6	7	5	3	1	22

Statistics

4

Number defective	4	5	6	7	8	9	Total
Frequency	1	4	5	2	2	1	15

5

Power, kW	1.1 – 1.2	1.2 – 1.3	1.3 – 1.4	1.4 – 1.5	1.5 – 1.6	Total
Frequency	3	4	7	5	1	20

Part 3 Display of data

1 **a** 1983, 1984, 1985

b 50 males, 45 females

c

Year	1981	1982	1983	1984	1985
Number of male	60	50	30	25	15
Number of female	50	45	45	35	20
Yearly total	110	95	75	60	35

d There is a gradual decline in the number of new recruits, more severe amongst the male trainees.

2 **a** 12th January

b 6th January

c 4th-5th January

d 8th-9th January

3 **a** 1983, 1984

b 1981

c £$2\frac{1}{2}$ million

d 1982

e Both home and export sales rose and declined over this period, with the trend in exports lagging one year behind the trend in home sales.

4 **a** 35

b 25

c 125

d 20%

5

Occupation	Angle	Fraction of total	Number of school-leavers
Employed	45°	$\frac{1}{8}$	30
Further Education	60°	$\frac{1}{6}$	40
Higher Education	45°	$\frac{1}{8}$	30
Youth Training	120°	$\frac{1}{3}$	80
Unemployed	90°	$\frac{1}{4}$	60
Total	360°	1	240

6

Land usage	Area (hectares)	Fraction of total	Angle
Arable	80	$\frac{1}{3}$	120°
Pasture	60	$\frac{1}{4}$	90°
Woodland	60	$\frac{1}{4}$	90°
Waste	40	$\frac{1}{6}$	60°
Total	240	1	360°

7

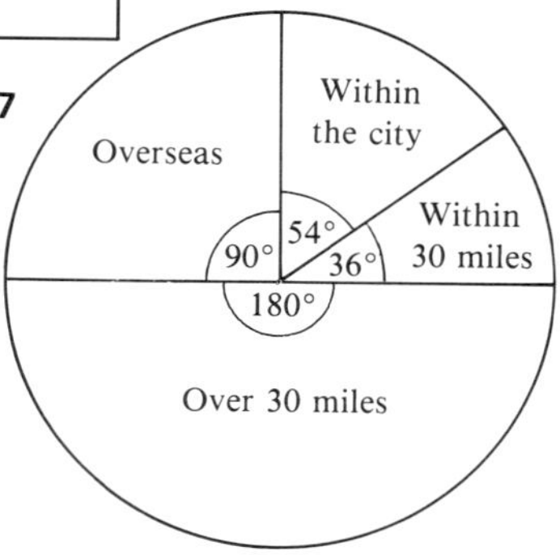

Statistics

8 **a** The advertisement does not state if the figures were produced by a reputable and impartial poll. The vertical axis is labelled only from 30% to 35% so that Mr. Hortayer's rise in support from $31\frac{1}{2}\%$ to $33\frac{1}{2}\%$ is exaggerated. A 2% rise between May and October hardly indicates 'support rising fast', and might be a result only of the errors incurred in the sampling process. August and September are omitted from the axis so the graph indicates a faster rise than actually occurs.

b The height of the columns indicates the percentage of real meat, and Wilson's percentage (about 80%) is only slightly more than the 'others'. Yet, Wilson's column is much wider than 'others' so that its area gives the impression of a much greater percentage in Wilson's burgers. The pictures of fat and lean cows emphasise the same point.

c 25% per annum for 4 years is not 'easy terms'. Depending on how the loan is arranged, it could involve a total repayment cost of between £5000 and £6000. The pile of coins does not indicate almost a doubling of the cash price if hire purchase is used.

9 **b** about 13 cm

10 **a** about 18 000 visitors

11 **a** There seems to be little correlation from the graph.

b no

Part 4 Measures of average and of spread

1

	a	**b**	**c**
Mode	1	4	2
Median	1	8.5	4
Mean	1.5	9.6	4.8

2 **a** Mode = 0
Median = 0
Mean = 4.5 mm

b No; reject the mode and median; the mean is the most useful in this case.

3

	a	**b**	**c**
Mode	1	0	4
Median	2	2	4
Mean	2.5	1.8	4

4 **a** Mode = 2 days, Mean = 4.9 days

b Mode = 13, Mean = 11.3

5

	Modal class	Estimate of mean
a	1000 – 1500	1303
b	10-15 kg	14.7 kg
c	$3 - 3\frac{1}{2}$ min	3.25 min
d	130 – 140 litres	130.7 litres

6 9

7 150

8 2

9 28

10 £140

11 **a** Median = 72.5%
Lower quartile = 66%
Upper quartile = 80%

b (i) Range = 34%
(ii) Interquartile range = 14%

			Mrs Kaye	Mrs Lamb	Mrs McPhee
12	**a**	Median	9	10.5	10
	b	Lower quartile	7	8	9
		Upper quartile	12	11	12
	c	Interquartile range	5	3	3
	d	Range	7	6	6

Statistics

			Excell	*Powerite*
13	**a**	Median	37 h	$37\frac{1}{2}$ h
	b	Range	27 h	41 h
	c	Lower quartile	26 h	35 h
		Upper quartile	$44\frac{1}{2}$ h	41 h
		Interquartile range	$18\frac{1}{2}$ h	6 h

d The battery only lasted 2 hours.
Excell

e Interquartile range

f Powerite

14 **b** (i) Median = 2.07 kg (ii) Lower quartile = 2.02 kg
Upper quartile = 2.14 kg
(iii) Interquartile range = 0.12 kg

15 **a** 5.6 **b** 3, 8.4
c 5.4

16 **a** (i) 9.4 h (ii) 6.4 h, 11.6 h
(iii) 5.2 h
b (i) 9.1 h (ii) 6.3 h, 11.0 h
(iii) 4.7 h
c Although Drayton Bay has the higher median, Whitbeach has the lower interquartile range. The choice is therefore Whitbeach.

17 **a** 60
b 45
c 30
d 80

18 **b** 84
c 84

19 **b** 450
c It continues in operation.

A mixture of short problems

Part 1

1 £7035

2 £230

3 16.05

4 15

5 **a** $\frac{3}{5}$
b 60%

6 **a** 15 km **b** 32 m

7 **a** 464 kg **b** 460 kg

8 **a** $\frac{1}{6}$ **b** $\frac{1}{3}$

9 $p = 50°$, $q = 80°$, $r = 80°$

10 **a** 10
b 4

11 **a** (i) $1\frac{3}{8}$ inch
(ii) $\frac{3}{10}$ square inches
b 16 m

12 £9·80 (including postage)

13 **a** $x = 4\frac{1}{2}$ **b** $x = 16$

14 **a** 1.2 km
b 700 cm^3
c 6 m^2

15 **a** $V = 18$ cm^3
b $L = 32$ m

16 £7011

17 Laura: £2500
Mary: £3750
Nicola: £8750

18

	t	0	1	2	3	4	5
a	$y = 2t + 1$	1	3	5	7	9	11
b	$y = \frac{1}{2}t + 7$	7	$7\frac{1}{2}$	8	$8\frac{1}{2}$	9	$9\frac{1}{2}$

d 4 minutes

19 **a** 42 m^2
b 80 m^2
c 148 m^2
d £207·20

20 **a** 21 metres
b 64.5°

21 **a** 4710 cm^3
b 6600 grams

A mixture of short problems

22 *Total cost of petrol, £*

	Garage *A*	Garage *B*
Rentet	133	136
Quickar	130	135

23

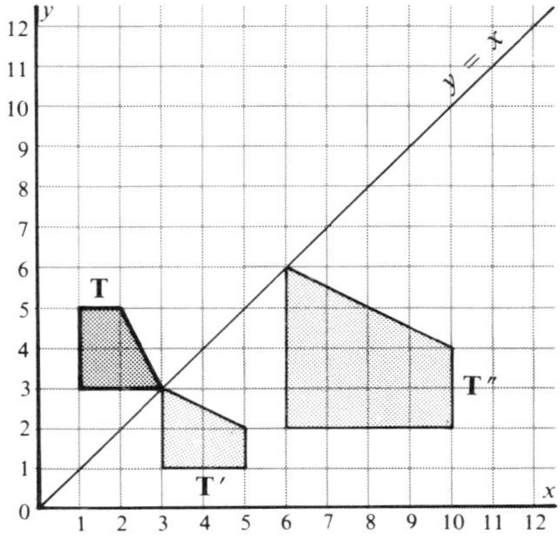

24 **a** 09.56
b 13.01
c 10 minutes

25 **a** Monday and Tuesday
b 12, 12, 10, 14, 15°C
Mean = 12.6°C
c Tuesday
d Friday

26

	Name of shape	Number of faces F	Number of vertices V	Number of edges E	F + V − E
a	Cuboid	6	8	12	2
b	Pyramid	5	5	8	2
c	Tetrahedron	4	4	6	2
d	Triangular prism	5	6	9	2
e	Cylinder	3	0	2	1

Solid **e** is the only solid with a curved surface.

27 **a** 16 22
b 37 50
c 216 343

28 8 sides

29 **a** 20.8 miles
b 102°

30 **a**

Number of pieces	4	9	16	25
Number of cuts	2	4	6	8

b 169 pieces

Part 2

1 **a** $9\frac{1}{2}$ h
b £38

2 **a** £6·74
b £60·66

3 **a** $\frac{11}{20}$
b 55%

4 **a** $\frac{5}{8}$ inch
b $1\frac{1}{2}$ square inches

5 **a** 2.44 gallons
b 20 bottles

6 E = 1800 joules

7 **a** 5.55 miles
b 6 miles

8 £2·32

9 **a** 754 cm^3
b 7 cm

10 a = 7 cm
b = 4 cm
c = 12 cm
d = 13 cm
e = 13 cm
f = 9 cm

11 $x = 70°$
$y = 60°$
$z = 36°$

12 **a** $x = 2\frac{1}{2}$
b $x = 8$

13 **a** 300 m^2
b $\frac{1}{4}$

14 **a** 2 children
b $\frac{1}{10}$
c 20%
d 87; 2.9

15 **a** 24 cm^2
b 240 cm^3
c 1.68 kg

16

Time, min	1	2	5	10	25
Height of water, cm	$2\frac{1}{2}$	5	$12\frac{1}{2}$	25	$62\frac{1}{2}$

12 minutes

A mixture of short problems

17 Jean £1800
Kate £3600
Laura £3600

18

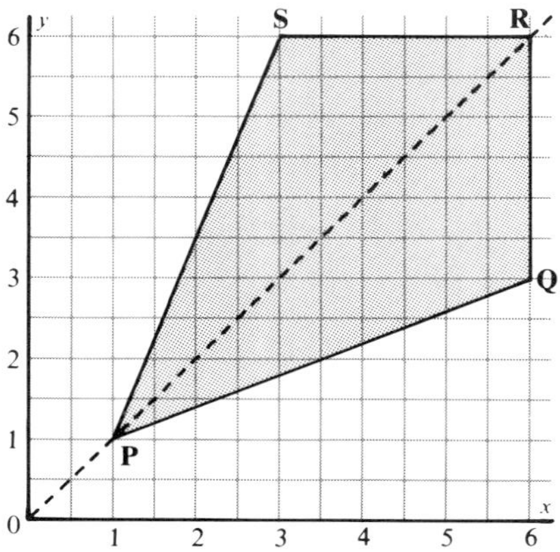

a a kite
b $y = x$
c 15 square units

19 **b** 8.7 km
c 105°

20 **a** 5 km
b 23 km

21 **a** 5 and 6
b $\frac{1}{10}$
c 12 times

22 **a** Centre (2, 3)
b 90° clockwise

23 **a** $m = 7$
b $n = -8$

24 **a** 3
b 27
c 3240 litres

25 **a** 35 minutes
b It does not run on a Saturday.
c 09.39
d 55 minutes

26 30%

27 **a** 1.5 km
b 150 metres
c 5.7°

28 **a** 40 km/h
b $\frac{1}{4}$ h
c 60 km, $1\frac{1}{2}$ h
d 30 km/h
e $3\frac{3}{4}$ h

29 $x = 70°$

30 **a** 11 **b** 16

Part 3

1 **a** £60·90
b £3·08

2 £51·60

3 6%

4 **a** £12
b (i) £16
(ii) 6.4%
c £16·40

5 **a** 5
b 40 cm^3
c 12
d 88 cm^2

6 £71·63

7 **a** 1979
b 550 million
c 1981
d 1983, Mitushi's production had overwhelmed Etronco's.

8 13.25

9 $\frac{1}{10}$

10 $x = 70°$
$y = 72°$
$z = 45°$

11 **a** 0 **b** 1 **c** 1.3

12 **a** $t = 5$
b $t = 4$
c $x = \frac{1}{2}at^2$

13 **a** $\frac{1}{13}$ **b** $\frac{1}{26}$ **c** $\frac{16}{52}$

14 **a**

	Units of Electricity	Units of Gas
Riley	360	200
Wood	150	380

Cost per unit in pence	
10	Electricity
14	Gas

b Riley £64
Wood £68·20

A mixture of short problems

15 **a**

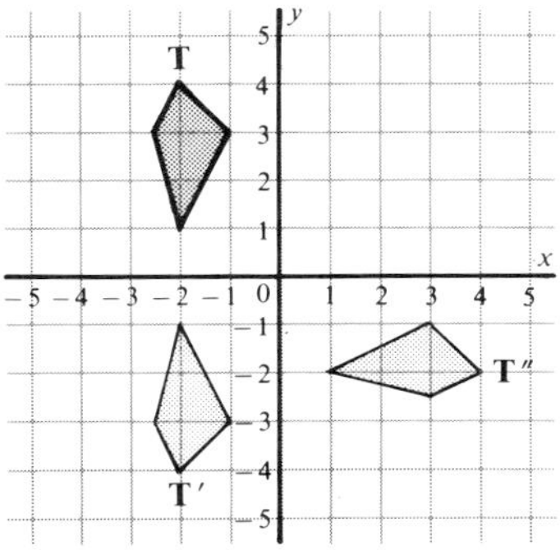

b A reflection in the line $y = x$.

16 **a** 50.3 cm^2
b 402 cm^3
c 110 cm^3

17 **a** 6.4 metres
b 51.3°

18 110.5 metres

19 **a** no
b Bristol and Cheltenham

20

Speed, mph	20	30	50	60	80
Time, h	6	4	2.4	2	1.5

Just over $3\frac{1}{2}$ h.

21 **a**

Number of kites	2	3	4	5	6	7	8
Number of triangles	2	4	6	8	10	12	14

b 98
c $2n - 2$
d 44

22 **a** 1:4:5
b 14 kg sileage; $17\frac{1}{2}$ kg kale
c 25 cows

23

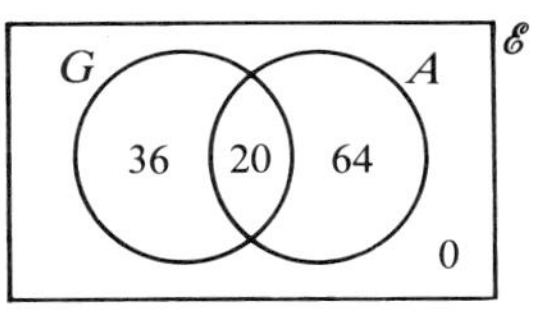

b 30%

24 **a** 6 rps anticlockwise
b 12 rps clockwise

25

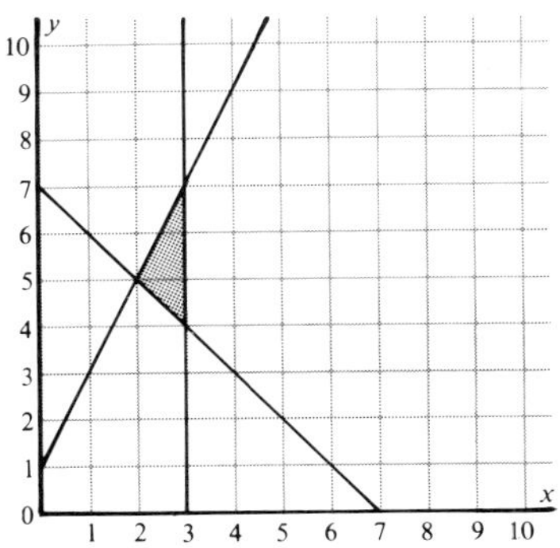

b $1\frac{1}{2}$ square units

26 **a** 5 km
b 15 km
c 225 km^2

27 **a** 12 cm
b 336 cm^2
c 360 cm^3

28 **a** **plan**

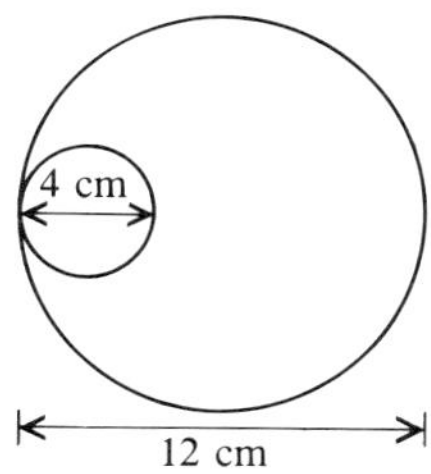

elevation

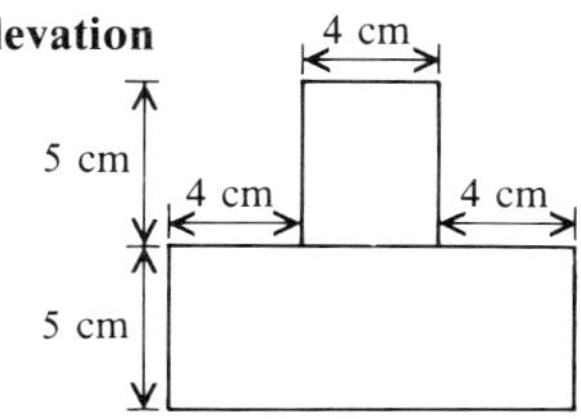

b 80 cm^2

29 **a** $x = 84°$
b $\frac{1}{5}$
c £48 million

30 **a** 81 cm^2
b 72 cm^2
c 103 cm^2

Costing problems

Part 1

1 **a** 84 m^2
b £71·40
c 4.2 m^3

2 **a** 21 litres; £9·66
b 84 km/h
c 4p/min

3 **a** 396 cm^3, 880 cm^3
b 0.47p/cm^3, 0.34p/cm^3
c The larger size is the 'better buy'.

4 **a** 110 m^2
b eleven times
c £1·32

5 **b** 326 m; £470
c 7000 m^2; £19 900
d about 151 days

6 **a** $33\frac{1}{2}$ h; £159·10
b £5·75 per hour; £74·75
c £233·85

7 **a** 16.40 should be altered to 11.40
b (i) 425 mph (ii) 453 mph
c 28 mph
d (i) 32p/min (ii) 4.5p/mile

8 **a**
  £94·50
+ £20·00
£114·50

b 147 m^2
c 10 tins; £24

9 **a** (i) £9750
(ii) £1410
b (i) £1560 (ii) £1620
c £540
d £4050
e £5700

10 **a** 9 m^3; £648
b 170 m^2
c £550
d £50

Part 2

1 **a** £171·20
b
  £171·20
  £21·40
+ £22·47
£215·07

2 **a** 72; £68·40
b 0.36 m^3; £3·06
c £75·03

3 **a** 10.5 m^3
b 2.46 m^3
c 50 bags; £63

4 **a** 5200 m^2
b £449 900
c £22 500

5 **a** £30·30
b £25·29
c £55·59
d 50.75 mph
e 7 miles/litre
f 5.27 pence/minute

6 **a** £124·80; £6·24
b £15·60; £28·08

7 **a** 592 attendances
b £80 + £118·40 = £198·40
c £163·28
d £72·54

8 **a** 15 m^2
b $2\frac{1}{2}$ m
c 96 m^2
d 11 litres
e 5 × 2 litres £44·50
1 × 1 litre £4·70
£49·20

9 **a** 27 m^2; 1890 bricks
b 2 loads needed; 110 bricks unused
c £216·20

10 **a** £481·64
b £19·27
c 364 500 lira
d £24·05

Part 3

1 **a** First £93·10; Second £69·12
b £82·62
c almost 9 hours

2 **a** 92 m^2
b (i) 25 tiles (ii) 2300 tiles
c £338·56

3 **a** 2.6 m^3
b 45p/litre
c 508 litres, £228·60

4 **a** 720 m^3
b 12 m^3
c 60 lorry loads
d £72

Costing problems

5 **a** £1380
b (i) £2580 (ii) £50
c £1920 + 480 = £2400
d Public transport (train and bus) by £180

6 **a** £557
b £13·93

7 **a** 72 tins; £23·04
b 352 cm^2
c 35.5 pence
d *First* 503 cm^3
Second 226 cm^3
e *First* gives 15.7 cm^3/p
Second gives 14.1 cm^3/p
The first tin is the 'better buy'.

8 **a** (i) £56·10 (ii) £112·80
b 2450 m^2; 122.5 m^3; £2940
c £3110

9 **a** 704 m^2
b 44 litres
c 4 × 10 litres = £100·00
2 × 2 litres = £11·20
Total cost = £111·20

10 **a** 2926 units; £163·86
b £171·31
c £59·92
d £64·53
e £46·86

A mixture of longer problems

Part 1

1 **a** 2.5 m, 4.33 m
b 5.4 m^2
c 120°
d 26.2 m^2
e 37.0 m^2
f 1850 m^3

2 **a** (i) 554 tonnes
(ii) 5.5 tonnes/ha
b 5.6 tonnes/ha

3 **a** (i) $x = 2\frac{1}{2}$ (ii) $x = 1\frac{1}{8}$
b $x = 55°$
c (i) x^2
(ii) $2x$
(iii) $x^2 + 2x$
(iv) $x = 4$ metres

4 **a** 8 m, 4 m
b 13.6 m
c 72.9°
d 34.2°

5 **a**

x	-1	$-\frac{1}{2}$	0	$\frac{1}{2}$	1	2	$2\frac{1}{2}$	3
x^2	1	$\frac{1}{4}$	0	$\frac{1}{4}$	1	4	$6\frac{1}{4}$	9
$-2x$	$+2$	$+1$	0	-1	-2	-4	-5	-6
$+2$	$+2$	$+2$	$+2$	$+2$	$+2$	$+2$	$+2$	$+2$
y	5	$3\frac{1}{4}$	2	$1\frac{1}{4}$	1	2	$3\frac{1}{4}$	5

b The equation has no solutions as the graph does not intersect the x-axis.
c $x = 2$

6 **b** R' (6, 4), (10, 4), (7, 1), (3, 1)
c R'' (−4, −1), (−4, −3), (−1, −3), (−1, −1)
d a reflection in the line $y = -x$; $\begin{pmatrix} 0 & -1 \\ -1 & 0 \end{pmatrix}$

7 **a** $x + y \geqslant 10$
b $x \geqslant 3$
$y \geqslant 2$
d $150x + 400y$
e 8 sheep and 2 cows; £2000

8 **a** 17.07
b Metroline 2; 10 minutes
c 17.12; a 10-minute wait
d Metroline 1; 17.14 from Gateshead
e Metroline 3; 51 minutes
f Metroline 3; 17.33 from Central Station, arriving at Whitley Bay at 17.58
g Metrolines 1 and 3; Heworth, Gateshead, Central Station, Monument, Haymarket, Jesmond, South Gosforth.
(i) 2 minutes
(ii) 7 minutes
(iii) 17.41 at Shiremoor
h Yes; depart Chichester at 16.45, arrive Benton at 17.23; Metrolines 1 and 2; a journey of 38 minutes.

A mixture of longer problems

9 **b** Centre (1, 2)
c angle of rotation 60°; $CP = 12$ cm; Arc $PP' = 12.6$ cm

10 **a** £182·40
b (i) £9·12
(ii) £59·85
(iii) £122·55
c (i) £6576
(ii) £4730
(iii) £1419
(iv) £5157

Part 2

1 **a** 6 m, 18.5 m
b 12.5 m
c 76.5°, 76.5°
d 52.1 m

2 **a**

x	3	4	5	6	7	8
$x-2$	1	2	3	4	5	6
y	6	3	2	1.5	1.2	1

b

x	2	4	6	8
y	1	2	3	4

c 460
d £1920

3 **a** (i) £12·68 (ii) £49·10
b x → Multiply by 3 → Subtract 2 → Square → Divide by 4 → y

$y = 25$
c (i) 2.4 ohms (ii) 0.53 ohms

4 **b** 31.7 km
c Area = 67 km^2; Cost = £42 000
d 5.4 km
450 metres; 4.8°

5 **a** $x = 40°$; $y = 35°$; $z = 25°$
b 65°
c (i) 12.20
(iii) 580 miles; 259°

6 **a** S' (3, −1), (4, −2), (3, −2), (2, −1)
b S'' (4, 2), (4, 4), (2, 4), (2, 2)
c Area of S' = 1 square;
Area of S'' = 4 squares;
Area scale factor = 4
d Enlargement of length scale factor 2 and centre the origin; $\begin{pmatrix} 2 & 0 \\ 0 & 2 \end{pmatrix}$.

7 **a**

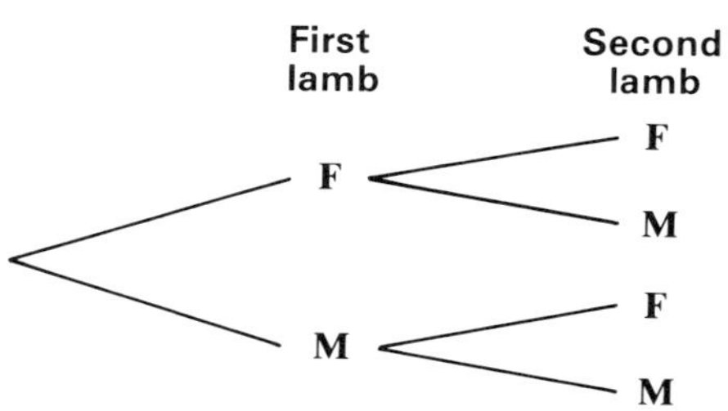

P (two male lambs) = $\frac{1}{4}$

b

Time, minutes	10.0 – 10.9	11.0 – 11.9	12.0 – 12.9	13.0 – 13.9	14.0 – 14.9	
Midpoint of class	10.45	11.45	12.45	13.45	14.45	Total
Number of pigeons	4	2	8	4	2	20

(i) Modal class is 12.0 – 12.9 minutes
(ii) 247 minutes; 12.35 minutes
(iii) $\frac{6}{20} = 0.3$

A mixture of longer problems

8 **a** 0.52 m^2
b 16.04 m^2
c 0.80 m^3
d 0.24 m^3

9 **a** (i) $\frac{1}{4}$
(ii) $\frac{1}{16}$
(iii) 5 m^2
b Centre (3, 4); 90° clockwise
c (i) OUZ
(ii) OWV
(iii) OXW
(iv) OZU
(v) XYO
(vi) WOV
(vii) VOU

10 **a** (i) £1440
(ii) £5760
(iii) £480
b (i) Possible loans are £21 600 and £29 000.
Greater loan equals $2\frac{1}{2}$ times joint income.
(ii) £31 500
(iii) £2880
(iv) £2160
(v) £17 280

Part 3

1 **a** 7.1 cm^2
b 1136 cm^3; 1.136 litres
c 49 000 litres
d 7 metres

2 **a** 2.24 metres
b 10.96 m^2
c 4.12 metres
d 4.58 metres
e 25.9°

3 **a** $x + y \leqslant 500$
b $y \leqslant x$
c $x \leqslant 350$
d Corner points are (0, 0), (250, 250), (350, 150), (350, 0)
e Maximum income of £1250 when $x = 250$ and $y = 250$.

4 **b** AB = 60 km; speed = 20 km/h
c BC = 50 km; time taken = 2.5 h
d OC = 73 km; speed = 29.2 km/h
Time of interception is 17.10 h

5 **a** Area =

$$\begin{array}{r} 750 \\ 1500 \\ 500 \\ 600 \\ +\,1000 \\ \hline 4350 \text{ m}^2 \end{array}$$

b QT = 92 m; Area of track = 368 m^2
c £2480
d 8.5%

6 **a** R_1 (6, −2), (14, −6), (16, −6), (8, −2)
b Area of R = 2 squares
Area of R_1 = 8 squares
Area scale factor = 4
c R_2 (1, 1), (1, 3), (2, 3), (2, 1)
d $NM = \begin{pmatrix} 1 & 0 \\ 0 & 1 \end{pmatrix}$
"The matrix N is the *inverse* of matrix M".

A mixture of longer problems

7 **a** For $y = 8x - x^2$:

x	0	1	2	3	4	5	6	7	8
$8x$	0	8	16	24	32	40	48	56	64
$-x^2$	0	−1	−4	−9	−16	−25	−36	−49	−64
y	0	7	12	15	16	15	12	7	0

For $y = \frac{1}{2}x$:

x	0	1	2	3	4	5	6	7	8
y	0	$\frac{1}{2}$	1	$1\frac{1}{2}$	2	$2\frac{1}{2}$	3	$3\frac{1}{2}$	4

On hitting the hillside at P, the ball is $3\frac{3}{4}$ metres vertically above O and $7\frac{1}{2}$ metres horizontally from O.

b 76.0°

8 **a** a reflection in the line $y = x$

b 153 cm^2

c (i) 5 cm; 60°
(ii) angle of rotation is 30° clockwise
(iii) 28 cm^2

9 **a** £280 + £95 = £375

b 250 × 4.80 = 1200 francs

c 54 × 14 × 8 = 6048 francs

d Total cost = £979
Cost per person = £122
e.g. Insurance and entertainment

10 **a** to the left

b on the right

c to the right

d $\frac{1}{4}$ minute, entering Beeston Road

e 1500 m/min, approx. 55 miles per hour

f 600 m/min

g A 1, B 4, C 5, D 6, E 7, F 9

h 3000 m/min^2

i approximately 3300 metres; 660 m/min

Aural exercises

Pupils should have nothing available except pen or pencil and blank paper when answering these questions. The questions in the second half of each exercise require pupils to refer to the tables and diagrams in the last section of their text book.

Each question should be read twice to the pupils and an adequate time allowed for them to answer without any sense of haste. If pupils need to jot down any item of information, they should do so on the same sheet of paper. However, no written calculations should be carried out and the use of calculators is not allowed.

Aural exercises

Exercise 1

1 You buy a magazine costing thirty nine pence and give the shopkeeper a fifty-pence piece. What change do you receive? *(11 pence)*

2 I usually go to work by bus and the journey takes me one hour. If I get a lift in a friend's car, I get to work three times as fast. How long does the journey take when I get a lift in the car? *(20 min)*

3 I go into a cafe with some friends and buy five sandwiches at twenty one pence each. What is the total cost? *(£1·05)*

4 A carpet is two metres wide and six and a half metres long. What is its area? *(13 m^2)*

5 I arrive at the station twelve minutes before the train is due to leave. However, the train is running seven minutes late. How long do I have to wait before I set off on the train? *(19 min)*

6 A car's mileometer shows that the car has travelled sixty four thousand and ninety seven miles. Write down the number sixty four thousand and ninety seven. *(64 097)*

7 John Brewer lives with his parents. He gives them two thirds of what he earns. If he earns sixty pounds each week, how much of this does he give to his parents? *(£40)*

8 When I woke up this morning, the outside temperature was minus two degrees Celsius. By the time I had finished my breakfast, the temperature had risen to three degrees Celsius. How many degrees had the temperature risen? *(5 °C)*

9 Miss Parry earns two pounds and ninety five pence per hour. She works a forty-hour week. What is her approximate basic weekly wage? *(£120 approx, £118 exact)*

10 I have a ball of string six metres long. How many pieces of string twenty centimetres long can I cut from it? *(30 pieces)*

The pupils will now need to turn to the last section of their textbook.

11 Turn to Table B.
How much is the total cost when you order two Kodacolor 126 (twenty-four exposure) films and one Quicksnap 135 (twenty-four exposure) film? *(£5·40)*

12 Turn to Table G.
You go on holiday to France and change ten pounds sterling into French francs. How many francs do you get? *(105.8 francs)*

13 Turn to Diagram L.
Estimate the size of this angle in degrees. *(80°)*

14 Turn to Table N.
You catch the half-past-nine morning train from Longbridge. How many minutes before ten o'clock do you arrive at Birmingham New Street Station? *(7 mins)*

15 Turn to Table I.
You are going on a business trip to Singapore. How much cheaper is it to buy one return ticket rather than two separate single tickets? *(£20)*

16 Turn to Diagram F.
What reading is given by arrow **a** on this scale? *(18)*

17 Turn to Diagram P.
This diagram shows the net of a solid. Describe the solid in one or two sentences. *(a square-based pyramid)*

18 Turn to Table Y.
The programme 'Newsnight' begins at ten thirty five. How many minutes is it before the next programme starts? *(45 mins)*

19 Turn to Diagram H.
This diagram shows a cube with one corner removed. How many edges does the remaining solid have? *(15 edges)*

20 Turn to Table U.
This table shows the amounts you have to repay if you take a loan from a finance company. You borrow six and a half thousand pounds. If you repay the loan over seven years (that is, over eighty four months), what is the total amount which you repay? *(£10 832·64)*

Aural exercises

Exercise 2

1 What is the cost of four boxes of chocolates at one pound twelve pence each? *(£4·48)*

2 I catch a train at half past two and arrive at my destination at twelve minutes to three. How long did my journey take? *(18 mins)*

3 Canute, King of England and Denmark, died in the year one thousand and thirty five. William of Normandy became King of England in the year one thousand and sixty six. How many years separated these two events? *(31 years)*

4 The houses on a certain street are numbered only with consecutive even numbers. No house has an odd number. How many houses are there between number sixteen and number thirty two? *(7 houses)*

5 Mrs Woodall has a sugar bowl which can hold three-quarters of a kilogram of sugar. How many times can she fill the bowl from a three-kilogram bag of sugar? *(4 times)*

6 It is thirty six miles from my home to York. If I average a speed of eight miles per hour on my bicycle, how long will it take to get to York? *($4\frac{1}{2}$ hours)*

7 A television is advertised at a price of two hundred pounds plus VAT. How much VAT do you have to pay if it is charged at fifteen per cent? *(£30)*

8 Mrs Yates earns four pounds an hour. When she works overtime, she earns 'time-and-a-half'. Yesterday she worked two hours overtime. How much did she earn for this overtime? *(£12)*

9 The outside temperature is six degrees Celsius. If it drops by ten degrees, what will the temperature be? *(−4°C)*

10 A new car tyre costs forty one pounds eighty seven pence. What is the approximate cost of three of these tyres? *(£126)*

The pupils will now need to turn to the last section of their textbook.

11 Turn to Table A.
You are going to fly from Manchester to Glasgow and back on North British Airlines. How much cheaper is it to buy a return ticket rather than two separate single tickets? *(£20)*

12 Turn to Diagram D.
This diagram shows an L-shaped solid. How many faces has it? *(8 faces)*

13 Turn to Table K.
This advertisement shows various holidays organised by Superdeal. From which airport are holidays to Ibiza available for both seven nights and fourteen nights? *(Birmingham)*

14 Turn to Diagram R.
Write down an estimate of the size of this angle in degrees. *(120°)*

15 Turn to Diagram X.
Write down the reading on this scale indicated by the arrow labelled **a**. *(4.2)*

16 Turn to Table O.
You are going to make a telephone call to your cousin in the USA which will last for five minutes. Calls to the USA are priced in charge band D of this table. How much more expensive is it if you telephone at the standard rate rather than the cheap rate? *(92 pence)*

17 Turn to Diagram S.
This diagram shows a square of area one square centimetre and also an irregular shape Write down an estimate of the area of the irregular shape in square centimetres. *(about 11 cm^2)*

18 Turn to Diagram Q.
This map shows the part of Cornwall nearest to Land's End. Starting from St. Ives, you go on the roads shown on the map to finish at Land's End. How many different routes are there from St. Ives to Land's End without travelling on the same road twice? *(6 routes)*

19 Turn to Table V.
Mr and Mrs Aswat are to take their car on the ferry. They make a return booking and return fares are double the single fares. They are charged on tariff C. Their car has a length of under four metres. What will they have to pay in total for themselves and their car for return tickets? *(£122)*

20 Turn to Diagram W.
This diagram shows the net of a solid. Describe the solid in one or two sentences. *(a triangular prism)*

Aural exercises

Exercise 3

1 Your electricity meter reading is seventy thousand, three hundred and sixty five. Write this number down in figures. *(70 365)*

2 The timetable says that the bus leaves at fourteen fifty two. The time now is twenty minutes to three. How long do I have to wait? *(12 mins)*

3 How much will it cost to carpet your bedroom at four pounds per square metre? The room is five metres long and three metres wide. *(£60)*

4 How many edges has a cube? *(12 edges)*

5 The journey by car from Bristol to Liverpool is all on motorway. If you average a speed of around sixty miles per hour, approximately how long will it take for the one hundred and eighty miles of the journey? *(3 hours)*

6 I take medicine regularly on my doctor's instructions. I use two-thirds of a bottle of medicine every month. How many bottles do I use in one year? *(8 bottles)*

7 What change do I get from a five-pound note if I buy three tins of oil at ninety seven pence each? *(£2·09)*

8 What is the approximate total cost of forty eight dresses at thirty two pounds each? *(£1500 approx, £1536 exact)*

9 The colliery in my home town closed down two years before my grandfather was born. He died five years ago at the age of sixty eight. How many years ago did the colliery close? *(75 years)*

10 A restaurant serves glasses of wine. Each glass holds seventy five millilitres. How many glasses can be served from a bottle holding three-quarters of a litre of wine? *(10 glasses)*

The pupils will now need to turn to the last section of their textbook.

11 Turn to Table G.
A businessman returns from Japan and gives his son a one-thousand-yen note. Approximately how much is the note worth in pounds sterling? *(£4)*

12 Turn to Diagram F.
Write down the reading on this scale indicated by the arrow labelled **b**. *(24)*

13 Turn to Diagram D.
This diagram shows an L-shaped solid. How many edges has this solid? *(18 edges)*

14 Turn to Table K.
You are thinking of going on holiday to Majorca, leaving from either Gatwick or Luton airport on the twenty fourth of July. How much extra do you have to pay if you decide to go for fourteen nights rather than seven nights? *(£60)*

15 Turn to Table N.
You just miss the eleven-fifty-eight train from Longbridge to Four Oaks. At what time does the next train leave Longbridge for Four Oaks? *(12.13)*

16 Turn to Table J.
You are going to post a letter weighing one hundred and forty two grams. How much will it cost to send by first-class post? *(32 pence)*

17 Turn to Diagram T.
This diagram shows the net of a cube. When the net is folded to make a cube, corners A and C come together. Which other corner also comes together with A and C? *(G)*

18 Turn to Table Y.
You are going on a trip tomorrow and you want to listen to the weather forecast on BBC2. You switch on the television at half past five and just miss the weather forecast. How long is it before there is another forecast on this channel? *(5 h 50 min)*

19 Turn to Diagram Q.
Write down as a three-figure number the approximate bearing of St Just from Land's End. *(030°)*

20 Turn to Diagram Z.
Which one of the four angles A, B, C and D is the biggest angle in this quadrilateral? *(Angle B)*

Aural exercises

Exercise 4

1 What is the cost of six magazines at twenty three pence each? *(£1·38)*

2 Atomic bombs were dropped on Hiroshima and Nagasaki in nineteen hundred and forty five. How many years ago was this? *(42 years, as of 1987)*

3 My rates bill is two hundred and forty pounds. The council are offering a discount of five per cent if I pay promptly. How many pounds is this discount worth? *(£12)*

4 How many corners has a cube? *(8 corners)*

5 I buy a tin of paint for sixty four pence with a one-pound coin. I receive thirty four pence change. By how much is the change incorrect? *(2 pence short)*

6 The outdoor temperature at three o'clock in the afternoon was eight degrees Celsius. By midnight it had fallen by twelve degrees. What was the temperature at midnight? *(−4°C)*

7 I walk at an average speed of two and a half miles per hour. How long will it take me to walk fifteen miles? *(6 hours)*

8 Annette Stubbs earns four pounds and ninety six pence per hour. What are her approximate earnings for a thirty-eight-hour week? *(£190 approx, £188·48 exact)*

9 A plastic container holds orange juice and is cuboid in shape. What volume in litres will be printed on its label if it is twenty centimetres long, ten centimetres wide and ten centimetres high? *(2 litres)*

10 A square carpet has an area of thirty six square metres. What distance is it right round the edge of the carpet? *(24 metres)*

The pupils will now need to turn to the last section of their text book.

11 Turn to Table A.
Mrs McDonald and her daughter, Fiona, make a single journey from Islay to London Heathrow. Fiona travels for half the normal single fare. What is the total amount which has to be paid for both of them? *(£123)*

12 Turn to Table I.
Mr Epstein flies to New York from London, but he flies back to Britain from Boston. He purchases two single tickets at the prices given in this table. What is the total amount he pays for the two tickets? *(£255)*

13 Turn to Table U.
You borrow five thousand pounds at the rates given in this table. What are your monthly repayments if you decide to repay the loan over a ten-year period? *(£86·65)*

14 Turn to Diagram E.
The rectangle drawn here has a width of two centimetres. Write down an estimate of its area in square centimetres. *(12 cm^2)*

15 Turn to Diagram X.
Write down the reading on this scale indicated by the arrow labelled **b**. *(5.8)*

16 Turn to Table O.
Mrs Westerby's daughter has gone on a school trip to Italy. Telephone calls to Italy are priced in charge band B. Mrs Westerby telephones her daughter at the cheap rate. How much would a six-minute call cost her? *(£2·76)*

17 Turn to Diagram T.
This diagram shows the net of a cube. When the net is folded, which edge comes into contact with edge *FG*? *(CD)*

18 Turn to Diagram C.
Which one of these five angles is the biggest? *(b)*

19 Turn to Diagram H.
This diagram shows a cube with one corner removed. How many faces has this solid? *(7 faces)*

20 Turn to Diagram Q.
This diagram shows a map of part of Cornwall. Which town is north-east of Treen? *(Penzance)*